James Fordyce

A Collection of Hymns and Sacred Poems

In two parts

James Fordyce

A Collection of Hymns and Sacred Poems
In two parts

ISBN/EAN: 9783744774901

Printed in Europe, USA, Canada, Australia, Japan

Cover: Foto ©Thomas Meinert / pixelio.de

More available books at **www.hansebooks.com**

A COLLECTION OF HYMNS AND SACRED POEMS,

IN TWO PARTS.

By JAMES FORDYCE.

Who reads with candour not to criticise,
Yet shews me friendly where an error lies:
Him as an honest faithful friend I'll love,
And studiously the useful hint improve:
For 'tis a maxim 'stablish'd firm with me,
To learn from ev'ry friend and book I see.

EDINBURGH:
Printed for the PUBLISHER.

MDCCLXXXVIII.
(Price 2s. in boards.)

PREFACE

THE following sheets were originally designed only for a few friends within the circle of my acquaintance, several of whom had for some time solicited me to select from among the metrical compositions I was possessed of, such favourite pieces as met with their esteem.

2. After I had arranged and digested the plan in which this Miscellany now appears, I communicated it to some friends, whose judgment of such productions I hold in the utmost veneration; who gave me to hope, if it was conducted agreeable to the manner I had adopted, it might, through Divine Grace, be more extensively useful.

3. In the selection of these Hymns, I have been industriously careful to admit of nothing which cherished or fomented doubtful disputations; no singular modes of opinion nor favourite peculiarities of a party are to be found here; nor any thing, in my humble opinion, that unbribed conscience, assisted by sanctified reason, can dissent from.

4. As to those Pieces of my own, which are thus distinguished ***, I can only say, that a love of poetry first induced me to compose and insert them; and I fear (as is frequently the case) without a previous inquiry whether or not I was sufficiently qualified for the undertaking.

5. However,

PREFACE.

5. However, if the candid reader thinks they may even have a remote tendency to improve the minds and morals of mankind, I hope the rectitude of my intentions will in some measure atone for the imbecillity of my performance, it being sufficiently obvious to numbers who have encouraged my attempts, that I lie under insurmountable disadvantages, which render it impossible for me to offer any thing to the eye of the learned or poetical critic, without being clothed with many imperfections; from these considerations 'tis humbly hoped the gentle reader will use rather the candour of a friend than the severity of a critic.

6. With a view of rendering the subsequent pages as useful as possible to the lower class of my readers, I have taken the liberty to subjoin an Alphabetical Table, containing an explication of such uncommon terms as are used in the following pages. The intelligent reader will easily see, and 'tis hoped, his candour will as easily pardon, the motives which induced me to adopt a plan so evidently calculated for the instruction of the meanest capacity.

7. That the Father of mercies may render the utility and advantage of this little book as extensive as its present circulation; That it may be a mean of instructing the ignorant, reclaiming the vicious, and of attracting the unthinking and unwary to the love of piety and virtue, is the sincere and ardent wish of the Publisher,

JAMES FORDYCE.

Edinburgh, Feb. 10. 1788.

CONTENTS

OF THE

HYMNS.

                                                        Hymn

*H*YMNS *on the Love,*   -   -   42, 50, 164
      Power,   -   -   22, 94, 152
Holiness,   -   -   -   75, 94
Goodness,   2, 8, 11, 41, 43, 85, 138, 166, 169
Wisdom,   -   -   -   -   6
Faithfulness,   -   -   -   142
And *Patience of God.*   -   145, 164
On the Creation,   -   12, 60, 96, 159
Redemption,   -   -   10, 79
Sanctification,   -   -   -   13
Preservation,   -   36, 70, 91, 97, 177
Justification,   -   -   89, 90
And *Glorification of Man thro' Christ.*   -   63
On the Incarnation,   -   -   86, 143
Life,   -   -   -   -   98
Sufferings,   -   67, 105, 126, 139
Crucifixion,   -   15, 95, 111, 129, 157
Resurrection,   -   -   77, 82, 84
Ascension,   -   -   17, 35, 139
And *Intercession of Christ.*   71, 121
On Faith,   -   -   89, 90, 119, 171
Repentance,   -   -   -   20, 161
Charity,   -   -   -   135
Humility,   -   24, 76, 87, 130, 132, 161
Happiness,   -   -   -   149
Affliction,   4, 7, 44, 109, 115, 117, 124, 137
Evening,   -   47, 69, 74, 120, 141, 153
                                              Morning,

	Hymn
Morning, —	65, 114, 120, 131, 175
Youth, — —	3, 25, 55, 80, 170
Old age, —	34, 73, 148, 165, 178
Sickness, —	72, 73, 127
Death, 16, 18, 31, 46, 93, 100, 101, 102, 107, 154	
Judgment, —	3, 32, 62, 64, 108, 126, 172
Heaven, — —	14, 51, 59, 81, 129, 163
Hell, — — — —	26, 92, 122
Scriptures, — —	48, 125, 147, 162
Public Worship, 5, 21, 27, 38, 40, 61, 68, 88, 102, 118, 134, 155, 160	
Prayer, — 29, 39, 112, 128, 144, 150, 156	
For Parents, — — — —	54, 57
Children, — — 3, 25, 55, 80, 170	
Masters, — — —	53, 176
Servants, — — —	52, 140
Mariners, — — 45, 56, 58, 133, 168	
Exiles and Captives, — —	113
Universal Praise to God, —	1, 30, 174
All my springs are in thee, Psal. lxxxvii. 7. —	9
Salvation, — — —	19
Temptation, — — —	23, 124
A Saint and Sinner's Dialogue, —	26
Sovereign Grace, — —	33
The Omnipresence of God, —	37, 151
For King George, — —	49
The Christian's Character, — —	66
The Attributes of God — —	99, 104
The Eternity of God, — —	106
The Gospel Trumpet, — —	110
The Immensity of God, — —	116
The Divinity and Humanity of Christ, —	123
The Hiding Place, Isa. xxxii. 2. —	146
A National Fast, — — —	158
Longing to be with Jesus, — —	167
Trust in God. — — —	173

'N. B. Those in *Italics* were expressed in the Proposals, the rest were not.

OF THE

POEMS.

	Page
PIETY and Politeness, a Dialogue,	142
The Creed versified,	149
A Soliloquy, written in a country church-yard,	150
The Decalogue in three versions,	153
The Lord's Prayer in six versions,	155
An Advice,—Benevolence,	160
An Estimate of human happiness,—On Repentance,	161
A Thought on sickness,	162
On Contentment,—Avarice and Ambition,	163
On Envy and Detraction,—The Life of Pleasure,	164
On Anger and Revenge,—Education,	ib.
Cruelty and Oppression,—The Grave,	165
The Vision, Job iv. 12,—21.	167
Rash Judgment,—Contentment,—Divine Power,	169
On Hope,	170
Universal Praise,	171
On Common Swearing,	172
On Compassion,	173
On Company,	174
On Jesus weeping over Lazarus' grave,	175
On Truth and Dissimulation,	ib.
Thoughts on Hell's torments, from Mat. xxv. 26.	ib.
———Heaven's happiness, from ditto	177
On Infidelity,	178
The Song of the Three Children paraphrased,	179
The xix. Psalm imitated,	205
Divine Foreknowledge,—A Morning thought,	206
A Complaint,—On Israel's Passage from Egypt,	207

On

	Page
On Divine Goodness,— A Call to Christian activity,	208
On Happiness,	209
Delusions detected,—On the phrase, "Killing Time,"	210
An ardent Wish,—A significant Hint,	211
An Epitaph,—On seeing the Sun rise,—On Eternity,	212
A Midnight Meditation,	213
On Pleasure,—On hearing a Passing Bell,	214
On Samuel's appearing to Saul,	ib.
On words and pronounciation,	215
The Criminal, an Elegy,	ib.
An Elegy on the Rev Mr G—d of C—d,	218
The First Psalm imitated,	219
The incomprehensibility of God, by G. K. Esq;	220
On Virtue,	222
On Modesty,—On Charity or Christian Love,	223
An Epitaph on an Infant,	ib.
An Ode, by the Rev. Mr J. T.—On Death,	225
On Ingratitude,—An Epitaph on Mrs * * *	227
A poetical inscription on a Nobleman's Pillar,	228
——————————— on his Lady's Pillar,	229
Captain ———'s excuse for not fighting a duel,	230
An Elegy, written in a Garden,	ib.
Divine Love,—An Ode,	231
On Riches,	232
For and against Life,	233
An Epitaph,—Mutual forbearance recommended,	234
The Power and Goodness of God,	235
On the Creation,	236
An Elegy to the Memory of Mrs Garden of Delgaty,	237
On being asked, what is the greatest blessing on earth?	240
The Widow's Son of Nain paraphrased, Luke vii. 11.	ib.
Time, part of an Elegy, written near Elgin Cathedral,	243
On the Death of a beautiful young Lady,	249
Moral Epigrams. On Friendship,—On Oeconomy,	251
On Vain Glory,—On Modern Friendship,	252
Thoughts on a Watch,	ib.

COLLECTION

OF

HYMNS.

HYMN I.

Universal Praise to God.

MY God, my King, thy various praise,
　　Shall fill the remnant of my days,
Thy grace employ my humble tongue,
Till death and glory raise the song.

2 The wings of ev'ry hour shall bear
Some thankful tribute to thine ear;
And ev'ry setting sun shall see
New works of duty done to thee.

3 Thy truth and beauty I'll proclaim,
Thy bounty flows, an endless stream;
Thy mercy swift, thine anger slow;
But dreadful to the stubborn foe.

4 Let distant times and nations raise
The long succession of thy praise:
And unborn ages make my song
The joy and labour of their tongue.

A　　　　　　　　5 But

5 But who can speak thy wond'rous deeds?
Thy greatness all our thoughts exceeds;
Vast and unsearchable thy ways,
Vast and immortal be thy praise.

II. *The Goodness of God.*

⁂ MY grateful soul to thee, O Lord!
    Presents its sacrifice;
O! let this feeble mite obtain
    Acceptance in thine eyes.

2 Thro' all the heedless steps of youth,
    When pride and passion reign'd;
Thy *grace* and *mercy* as my guide
    Did still my actions tend.

3 And when the cares of life approach'd,
    And still did multiply,
Thy unabated providence
    Did all my wants supply.

4 When e'er th' impending storm arose
    Of unexpected grief;
Thy pow'r and goodness were display'd
    To send me quick relief.

5 Now that the flaming torch of life
    Begins to waste apace,
Still in that goodness I'll confide
    That blest my former days.

6 How can I doubt thy guardian love,
    Or yet thy word distrust;
Whose name and nature still declare
    Thee merciful and just.

III. *Youth and Judgment.*

LO! the *young* tribes of Adam rise,
    And thro' all nature rove,
Fulfil the wishes of their eyes,
    And taste the joys they love.

2 They give a loose to wild desires;
    But let the sinners know,
The strict account that God requires
    Of all their works below.

3 The *Judge* prepares his throne on high,
    The frighted earth and seas
Avoid the fury of his eye,
    And flee before his face.

4 How shall I bear that dreadful *day*,
    And stand the fiery test?
I'd give all mortal joys away
    To be for ever blest.

IV. *Affliction.*

MY fainting soul to thee, O God!
    Breathes forth a plaintive sigh;
Deprest beneath affliction's rod,
    To thee for help I fly.

2 O Jesus! friend of sinners, hear
    My weak enfeebled cry;
Involv'd in pain, and grief, and fear,
    To thee for help I fly.

3 On thee I cast my burden, Lord,
    Do not my suit deny,
Invited by thy gracious word,
    To thee for help I fly.

4 Thou great Physician of my soul,
      Thou canst the cure apply,
And make a wounded sinner whole,
      To thee for help I fly.

5 All other springs of hope are gone,
      Their aid they all deny:
Dear Saviour, whilst I make my moan,
      To thee for help I fly.

6 On thee alone my faith lays hold;
      Thy word it cannot lie:
Divinely confident and bold,
      To thee for help I fly.

V. *Public Worship.*

COME let us join our cheerful songs,
      With angels round the throne;
Ten thousand, thousand are their tongues,
      But all their joys are one.

2 Worthy the Lamb that dy'd, they cry,
      To be exalted thus:
Worthy the Lamb our hearts reply,
      For he was slain for us!

3 Jesus is worthy to receive
      Honour and pow'r divine;
And blessings, more than we can give,
      Be, Lord, for ever thine.

VI. *The Wisdom of God.*

₊ DID not thy *wisdom* from above
      Conduct our steps in life;
Thy works on earth below—would prove
      A scene of jarring strife.

2 Thy creatures conftantly fulfil
    The ends to them affign'd;
Becaufe their tafk in *wifdom's* ftill
    Proportion'd to their kind.

3 Impell'd by thy fupreme command,
    The whole creation moves;
And ev'ry thing in fea and land,
    Thy boundlefs *wifdom* proves.

4 Whate'er is uniform or bright
    Beneath the fpreading fkies,
That gilds the morning or the night,
    Thy *wifdom* did devife.

5 Thy works throughout this fpacious ball
    Are great beyond compare;
"In *wifdom* haft thou made them all,"
    Thy goodnefs to declare.

VII. *Affliction.*

FATHER, I ftretch my hands to thee;
    No other *help* I know:
If thou withdraw'ft thyfelf from me,
    Ah! whither fhall I go.

2 What did thine only Son endure,
    Before I drew my breath!
What pain, what labour, to fecure
    My foul from endlefs death!

3 Author of faith, to thee I lift
    My weary longing eyes!
Preferve in me that gracious gift,
    My foul without it dies.

VIII. *The Goodness of God.*

⁂ ETERNAL source of love divine,
    From whom *all blessings* flow;
Angels in heaven sweetly join
    With saints on earth below:

2 With one consent their cheerful songs
    Aloft in anthems rise;
Thy praise employs the various tongues
    Of earth, and seas, and skies.

3 While the surrounding crowds proclaim
    His praise on ev'ry hand:
My soul, canst thou behold the same,
    And still inactive stand?

4 No! Lord, my feeble mite of praise
    Shall mingle with the crowd:
Thy matchless glory still to raise,
    My voice shall sound aloud.

5 Assist me all ye heav'nly pow'rs,
    Jehovah's praise to sing:
On wings of faith my spirit tow'rs
    To my eternal King.

IX. "*All my springs are in thee.*"—Psal. lxxxvii. 7.

NOW dearest Lord, to praise thy name
    Let all our pow'rs agree;
Worthy art thou of endless fame;
    Our springs are all in thee.

2 Here, in thy love, will we rejoice,
    All sov'reign, rich, and free;
Singing (we hope, with heart and voice)
    Our springs are all in thee.

3 To whom, dear Jesus, Oh! to whom
    Should needy sinners flee;
But to thyself. who bid'st us come?
    Our springs are all in thee.

4 Some tempted, weak, and trembling faint,
    Before thee now may be:
Let not his hopes nor courage faint;
    His springs are all in thee.

5 The poor supply, the wounded heal,
    Let sinners, such as we,
Salvation's blessing taste and feel;
    Our springs are all in thee.

6 When we arrive at Zion's hill,
    And all thy glory see;
Our joyful songs shall echo still,
    Our springs are all in thee.

X. *Redemption through Christ.*

⁂ WHEN unrelenting Justice cry'd
    For veng'ance on the fallen race,
Jesus our great *Redeemer* died,
    A bleeding victim in our place.

2 He in our stead resign'd his breath,
    His precious life for us he gave,
That from the jaws of endless death,
    He might us helpless sinners *save.*

3 The great Jehovah from above,
    Approv'd this spotless sacrifice:
By virtue of *redeeming* love,
    We find acceptance in his eyes.

4 Now that to *save* our souls from sin,
    He has this 'great salvation' wrought;
Let each of us resign to him
    The lives which he so dearly bought.

XI. *The Goodness of God.*

LORD, when I count thy *mercies* o'er,
    They strike me with surprise;
Not all the sands that spread the shore
    To equal numbers rise.

2 My flesh with fear and wonder stands,
    The product of thy skill;
And hourly *blessings* from thy hands
    Thy thoughts of *love* reveal.

3 These on my heart by night I keep;
    How kind, how dear to me!
O may the hour that ends my sleep,
    Still find my thoughts with thee.

XII. *The Creation.*

⁎ LORD, we admire thy mighty sway,
    Which into being brought our frame;
And has made animated clay,
    To praise the glory of thy name.

2 When o'er the undistinguish'd deep,
    Confusion spread her sable wings;
When all were silent and asleep,
    Earth's wide expanse to order *springs*.

3 The night and day, the sea and land,
    His unresisted pow'r disjoin'd;
And with his great and mighty hand,
    To each their function he assign'd.

4 That liquid mass, the spacious sea,
   He planted with the finny tribe;
And by a fencing hedge, you see
   Them wall'd around on ev'ry side.

5 The feather'd flocks of ev'ry kind,
   Still ranging in the purple sky,
With rapid wings, as swift as wind,
   Thro' their extensive empire fly.

6 Look round and view the terrene frame
   (See herds, with all the bleating race)
A splendid table, whereupon
   A rich profusion God doth place.

XIII. *Sanctification through Christ.*

BY nature vile, conceiv'd in sin,
   By practice render'd worse;
Deprav'd in ev'ry pow'r within,
   Obnoxious to thy curse.

2 I feel the weight and guilt of sin,
   My soul's with anguish torn;
Where shall I find a friend to screen
   A sinful rebel worm?

3 Methinks I hear some joyful sound,
   These words with love declare,
" Where tribulation most abound,
   My grace shall conquer there."

4 Jesus, my God! to thee I fly:
   Thy blood can *cleanse* from sin;
Thy righteousness † can all defy.
   'Tis thou canst make me clean.

† *Imputed and Implanted.*

5 Come, holy dove, inspire my soul,
  And ev'ry fear remove,
Let all my pow'rs in praises roll,
  And sing redeeming love.

XIV. *Heaven.*

*⁎*HOW blest is that angelic band,
  In robes of light who daily stand,
Who have at last obtain'd the grace,
To *see* unveil'd the "Prince of peace."
2 Their earthly trials now are o'er,
Their pain and grief are felt no more;
Join'd to the legions of the sky,
From earth and sin they quickly fly.
3 Above the reach of Satan's pow'r,
These disembodied spirits *tow'r*,
And on their dear Redeemer's breast,
From all their toils they safely rest.

XV. *The Crucifixion of Christ.*

BEHOLD the Saviour of mankind,
  Nail'd to the shameful tree;
How vast the love that him inclin'd
  To *bleed* and *die* for thee.
2 Hark how he *groans*, while nature shakes,
  And Earth's strong pillars bend!
The temple's veil in sunder breaks,
  The solid marbles rend.
3 'Tis done the precious ransom's paid,
  " Receive my soul," he cries;
See where he bows his sacred head!
  He bows his head, and *dies!*

4 But

4 But soon he'll break death's envious chain,
 And in full glory shine;
O Lamb of God was ever *pain*,
 Was ever *love* like thine.

XVI. *Death.*

⁂ OUR wasting days are rolling on,
 So swiftly glide away;
That unto our eternal home
 We hasten ev'ry day.

2 This moment, Lord, upon the brink
 Of *death*, we mortals stand;
And yet, alas! we seldom think,
 His darts so near at hand.

3 We fondly rove with heedless steps,
 In quest of idle toys;
Until, at once, *death* intercepts,
 And baffles all our joys.

4 The gaudy pomp of human pride,
 Unmask'd does then appear;
It's wings are cropt on ev'ry side,
 When *death* approaches near.

5 Since *death*, our bodies with the dust
 Appoints them their abode;
So *death* at last, we humbly trust,
 Will join our souls to God.

XVII. *The Ascension of Christ.*

HOSANNA to the prince of light,
 That cloath'd himself in clay;
Enter'd the iron gates of death,
 And tore the bars away.

2 Death is no more the king of dread,
  Since our Emmanuel rose;
He took the tyrant's sting away,
  And spoil'd our hellish foes.

3 See how the conqu'ror *mounts* aloft,
  And to his father flies!
With scars of honour in his face,
  And triumph in his eyes.

4 There our exalted Saviour reigns,
  And scatters blessings down:
Our Jesus fills the middle seat
  Of the celestial throne.

XVIII. *Death.*

⁎ JESUS, an int'rest in thy blood,
  This is my chief, my only care;
My pardon seal'd, and peace with God,
  Is still my undissembled pray'r.

2 Approaching *death* is just at hand,
  The lamp of life does fast decay;
And shall I waste my ebbing sand,
  And throw my inch of time away?

3 Great God! forbid the foolish thought,
  Permit it not to vex my heart:
That I whose life's so dearly bought,
  From Jesus' footsteps should depart.

  Jesus, beneath thy guardian wings,
    My fainting soul I safely hid;
And now, tho' *death* his warrant brings,
  I'll in thy precious blood confide.

XIX. *Salvation.*

SALVATION, O the joyful sound!
    What pleasure to our ears!
A sov'reign balm for ev'ry wound,
    A cordial for our fears.

2 Salvation! let the echo fly,
    The spacious earth around,
While all the armies of the sky,
    Conspire to raise the sound.

XX. *Repentance.*

JUSTLY incensed holy Lord,
Whose precepts I have long abhor'd;
Before thy throne may such as I
For pardon, Lord, to thee apply?

2 Deservedly thy vengeful pow'r,
Might sink me down, to rise no more;
Consign my guilty soul to hell,
There, in perpetual flames to dwell.

3 Before thee shall I perish, Lord?
Will Christ my soul no help afford?
Yet still methinks I hear thee say,
" Jesus can take thy guilt away."

4 O, gracious God, behold my cry!
Who gav'st thine only Son to die;
Forgiveness to my soul impart,
And write the pardon on my heart.

5 Then shall I spend my wasting days,
In sounding forth thy endless praise;
United to the saints above,
I'll shout with them Redeeming love.

XXI. *Public*

XXI. *Public Worship.*

IN boundless mercy gracious Lord appear,
  Darkness dispel, the humble mourner chear;
Vain thoughts remove, melt down *each* flinty heart,
Draw *ev'ry soul* to choose the better part.

XXII. *The Power of God.*

⁂ THE undesigning hand of chance,
    Could never into order bring,
The system of this wide expanse,
    With every created thing.

2 In these, O Lord, thy hand and pow'r
    Unveil'd are seen by mortal eyes;
Surrounding objects ev'ry hour,
    Proclaim thy *might* in earth and skies.

3 The atoms of this lofty frame,
    The human and angelic bands;
Forth from the womb of nothing came,
    Created by thy mighty hands.

4 Confusion into order wrought,
    Without miscarriage or defect;
And dust was to existence brought,
    By the *Almighty* Architect!

XXIII. *Temptation.*

GREAT God! who from my early youth,
  Hast form'd me by thy sacred truth,
Still guide me in thy righteous way,
Nor let me from thy precepts stray:

2 With *dangers* I'm encompass'd round,
And walk upon deceitful ground;
The world *allures*, the sense *invites*,
And promises unknown delights:

3 How can I pleasure's tide withstand,
Unless supported by thine hand?
Preserve unstain'd my innocence,
Or else in mercy call me hence.

XXIV. *Humility.*

⁎ NO temple ever built by art,
    Can Jesus Christ contain;
But in the *meek* and *humble* heart
    He's daily to be seen.

2 The man whose unaspiring mind,
    Submits to Jesus' rod,
His pious soul you'll always find
    A temple for his God.

3 No lawless passions mar his peace,
    No blasted hopes his joy:
His soul is fill'd with Jesus' grace,
    His pleasures never cloy.

4 Dear Saviour now this grace impart,
    Ambitious thoughts dispel:
Prepare a chamber in my heart,
    And there for ever dwell.

XXV. *Youth.*

THE morning flow'rs display their sweets,
    And gay their silken leaves unfold,
As careless of the noon-day heats,
    And fearless of the ev'ning cold.

2 Nipt by the wind's unkindly blast,
    Parch'd by the sun's directer ray,
The momentary glories waste,
    The short-liv'd beauties die away.

3 So blooms the human face divine,
　　When *youth* its pride of beauty shews:
Fairer than spring the colours shine,
　　And sweeter than the virgin rose.

4 But worn by slowly rolling years,
　　Or broke by sickness in a day,
The fading glory disappears,
　　Our *short-liv'd beauties* die away.

XXVI. *A Saint and Sinner's Dialogue.*

*** HOW can a guilty sinner shun
　　The death that never dies?
He must in faith and patience run
　　To Christ the Sacrifice.

2 How can my soul's polluted stains
　　(That still for veng'ance cry)
Be wash'd?—' The blood of Christ doth cleanse
　　From all iniquity.'

3 How shall my uninstructed heart
　　And life be kept from sin?
God's word the best of rules impart
　　To keep the conscience clean.

4 But how can Satan's fiery darts
　　Be warded off by me?
Resist him; and, for all his arts,
　　Unvanquish'd thou shalt be.

5 Will God his word to me fulfil,
　　Of this I stand in doubt?
Yes—' They that come to Christ, he will
　　In no ways cast them out.'

XXVII. *Public*

XXVII. *Public Worship.*

FATHER behold with gracious eyes
  The souls *before* thy *throne;*
Who now present their sacrifice,
  And seek thee in thy Son.

2 On each of us some gift bestow,
  Some blessing now impart,
The seed of life eternal sow
  In ev'ry *waiting* heart.

3 The loving pow'rful spirit shed,
  And speak our sins forgiv'n,
And haste throughout the lump to spread
  The sanctifying leav'n.

4 Refresh us with a ceaseless show'r
  Of graces from above,
Till all receive the perfect pow'r
  Of everlasting love.

XXVIII. *Hell.*

*** DESPAIR and darkness fill my heart,
  And tears run from mine eyes;
My pensive thoughts still call to mind
  The worm that never dies.

2 To be consign'd to endless pain,
  In flames of fire to dwell;
What mortal can endure the thought
  Of *Fiends,* and *Fire,* and *Hell.*

3 There, hope nor mercy never view
  Those tenants of despair;
But to endure redoubled pangs
  Their wretched souls prepare.

4 A guilty confcience lodg'd within,
    A vicious life behind,
A fin-avenging God above,
    Beneath a cruel fiend.

5 To 'fcape this endlefs wrath divine,
    Ah! whither can I flee;
O Jefus, fave me or I'm damn'd
    To all eternity!

XXIX. *Private Prayer.*

FATHER of Jefus Chrift, my Lord,
    I humbly feek thy face;
Encourag'd, by the Saviour's word,
    To afk thy pard'ning grace.

2 Ent'ring into my *clofet*, I
    The bufy world exclude;
In *fecret pray'r* for mercy cry,
    And groan to be renew'd.

3 Far from the paths of men, to thee
    I folemnly *retire:*
See thou, who doth in *fecret* fee,
    And grant my heart's defire.

4 Fain would I all thy goodnefs feel,
    And know my fins forgiv'n;
And do on earth thy perfect will,
    As angels do in heav'n.

XXX. *Univerfal Praife to God.*

**LET all that breathe the vital air,
    Unite with one accord,
A fong of praife, with joy, prepare
    To Chrift our common Lord.

2 Ye warbling *tenants* of the sky,
    Conspire to raise the sound;
Assist ye grazing *flocks* that lie,
    In pastures on the ground.

3 Ye *legions* of the deep combine,
    Your aid the rest desire;
And all ye *sons* of Adam join
    To swell the chanting choir.

4 Let *heav'n* and *earth* combine with *me*,
    The sacred theme to raise:
Let our united songs agree
    In great Jehovah's praise.

XXXI. *The departing Believer.*

LET ev'ry saint, and ev'ry friend,
    Rejoice and sing with me;
While I on angel's wings ascend,
    My Saviour's face to see.

2 *Adieu*, ye paths of death and sin,
    I soar to joys above;
Where I shall ever live with him,
    And sing redeeming love.

3 *Adieu*, my body, for a while;
    With me thou canst not go;
But mingle with thy native soil,
    Till the last trumpet blow.

4 Now Jesus calls my soul away,
    My flesh shall rest in hope:
When dawns the everlasting day,
    My Lord shall raise it up.

5 And as I mount, I'll louder sing
  Salvation through the skies,
And make the starry concave ring,
  With praises as I rise.

XXXII. *The Resurrection.*

WHEN the last angel's trump shall sound,
  And dreadful thunders roar;
The seas, and ev'ry grave around,
  Shall then their dead restore.

2 Then from the dark and silent bed,
  Where man has slept for years;
Some *rise* with joy to meet their head,
  And some with grief and fears.

3 The grave proves faithful to her trust,
  No more her slain conceals;
And those that mingled with the dust,
  Shall *quit* their gloomy cells.

4 The earth shall vanish into smoke,
  An unextinguish'd blaze,
The mountains melt, the solid rock,
  Dissolve as liquid seas.

5 Methinks the hour approaches nigh,
  The trumpet's sound I hear:
If heav'n and earth before thee fly,
  Lord, how shall I appear?

XXXIII. *Sov'reign Grace.*

ALMIGHTY Sov'reign of the skies,
  Lo, I present me at thy throne;
Fain would my soul enraptur'd rise,
  And sing the *wonders grace hath done.*

2 Ye humble fouls that love and fear,
   To Jefus' crofs with boldnefs run,
While I with joyful lips declare,
   The matchlefs *wonders grace hath done.*

3 Adore, my foul, the matchlefs *grace,*
   That taught thee folly's paths to fhun:
Let all thy pow'rs awake to praife
   The *wonders fov'reign grace hath done.*

4 And when this weak and dying frame
   Shall in the filent grave lie down,
Then in a more exalted ftrain,
   I'll tell the *wonders grace hath done.*

5 Join'd to the bleft angelic throng,
   That ftand adoring round the throne,
I'll fing, with an unwearied tongue,
   The matchlefs *wonders grace hath done.*

XXXIV. *Old Age.*

⁂ HOW foon the blooming flow'rs decay?
   Their beauty quickly fades away:
Their crimfon hue, their vernal green,
No more with pleafure can be feen.

2 So foon the fleeting moments pafs,
That ftill exhauft our mortal glafs;
From morn to noon, from youth to age,
We quickly fly from off the ftage.

3 In heedlefs fteps our youthful days,
Are fpent in fin and folly's ways:
Expended by the wreck of time,
Our ftrength and vigour foon decline.

4 Gray

4 Gray headed both in sin and years,
Old age with all his train appears;
Incumber'd with a load of pain,
We see our former actions vain.

5 And what in youth were pleasing joys,
We now esteem as idle toys;
Insensible of ev'ry smile
That does the cares of life beguile!

6 We, crush'd by sickness and distress,
Despair to find our burden less,
And grope about from year to year,
Until at last we disappear.

XXXV. *The Ascension of Christ.*

BEHOLD him triumph o'er the grave!
    Who once a victim stood;
Expos'd to wrath that we might have
    Salvation through his blood.

2 See him exulting *rise* on high,
    No more to weep and mourn;
Victorious see him *mount* the sky,
    To wait his grand return.

3 Celestial legions now attend,
    And in his train appear;
While myriads more from heav'n descend,
    To hail him through the air.

4 The heav'nly portals open wide,
    T' admit the conqu'ring God;
When tending seraphs, at his side,
    Resound his praise abroad.

5 Ye saints, exult in lofty strains,
   Your noblest tribute bring:
He lives, and shall for ever reign,
   The universal King!

XXXVI. *Preservation through Christ.*

*⁎*WHEN in the roaring lion's teeth,
      Depriv'd of help I lay;
Jesus, thou from the jaws of death
   Rescu'd the lawful prey.

2 My punishment thou didst sustain,
   On thee my sins were laid;
That I the blessing might regain,
   Accursed thou wast made.

3 Dear Saviour, how shall I discharge
   The debt I owe to thee?
Who as my surety did *enlarge*,
   And *bought* my *liberty*.

4 Thy heart for sinners still doth move,
   Thou suff'ring Son of God:
Descend in mercy from above,
   And cleanse me by thy blood.

5 Jesus, one blessing I require,
   Which thou hast bought for me;
Make this my great, my chief desire
   To live and die in thee!

XXXVII. *The Omnipresence of God.*

LORD, where shall guilty souls retire,
   Forgotten and unknown?
In hell they meet thy vengeful fire,
   In heav'n thy glorious throne.

2 Should I suppress my vital breath
    To 'scape the wrath divine,
Thy voice would break the bars of death,
    And make the grave resign.

3 If wing'd with beams of morning light,
    I fly beyond the west,
Thy hand, which must support my flight,
    Would soon betray my rest.

4 If o'er my sins I seek to draw
    The curtains of the night,
Those flaming eyes which guard thy law
    Would turn the shades to light.

5 The beams of noon, the midnight hour,
    Are both alike to thee:
O may I ne'er provoke that pow'r,
    From which I cannot flee!

XXXVIII. *Public Worship.*

*** JESUS, by thy redeeming blood
    In our behalf appear;
Thou dying suff'ring Son of God,
    We *wait* to meet thee here.

2 Inspire our souls with love divine,
    Melt down each flinty heart:
And by thy grace our wills incline
    To choose the better part.

3 The reigning pow'r of vice subdue,
    Thy work of grace begin;
'Tis thou alone that canst renew,
    And save our souls from sin.

4 That we our dear Redeemer love,
    Let all our actions shew,
Till glory ends in heav'n above
    What grace began below.

XXXIX. *A Prayer for Sinners.*

JESUS, Redeemer of mankind,
    Display thy saving pow'r,
Thy mercy let *these outcasts* find,
    And know *their* gracious hour.

2 Ah! give *them*, Lord, a longer space,
    Nor suddenly consume;
But let *them* take the proffer'd grace
    And flee the wrath to come.

3 Open their *eyes* and *ears*, to see
    Thy cross, to hear thy cries:
Sinner, thy Saviour weeps for thee,
    For thee he weeps and dies:

4 All the day long he meekly stands,
    His rebels to receive;
And shews his wounds and spreads his hands,
    And bids *you* turn and live!

XL. *Public Worship.*

. JESUS, thy glory we confess,
    Thy majesty adore,
Thy wisdom, truth, and holiness,
    We worship evermore.

2 Jesus, our dear redeeming Lord,
    Thy praise abroad we shew;
Be thou by heav'nly hosts ador'd,
    And all thy saints below.

3 Thy endless unabated love
    Is still to sinners free;
'Tis it alone that can remove,
    And help our misery.

4 Thy goodness and thy truth abound,
    A vast extensive sea,
Wherein our guilt and sin are drown'd
    To all eternity.

5 Jesus, thou Sun of Righteousness,
    In beams of mercy shine;
That so enlighten'd by thy grace,
    We may be ever thine.

XLI. *The Goodness of God.*

SWEET is the mem'ry of thy grace,
    My God, my heav'nly King!
Let age to age thy righteousness,
    In songs of glory sing.

2 God reigns on high, but not confines
    His *goodness* to the skies;
Thro' the whole earth his *goodness* shines,
    And ev'ry want supplies.

3 With longing eyes thy creatures wait
    On thee for daily food:
Thy lib'ral hand provides them meat,
    And fills their mouth with good.

4 How kind are thy compassions, Lord!
    How slow thine anger moves!
But soon he sends his pard'ning word,
    To cheer the soul he loves.

5 Creatures with all their endless race
    Thy pow'r and praise proclaim:
But we who taste thy richer grace,
    Delight to bless thy name.

XLII. *The Love of God.*

⁎ REJOICE ye ransom'd sons of men,
    Dispel your guilty fears;
The *love* of God (thro' Jesus shewn)
    In your behalf appears.

2 Such was his pity and his *love*,
    For Adam's fallen race,
He sent his Son from heav'n above,
    To suffer in their place.

3 Jesus to earth did not descend
    With a vindictive rod,
But to enforce, and recommend,
    And pave the way to God.

4 And they who love his holy word,
    And all his laws obey;
His *loving kindness* shall record,
    Thro' everlasting day.

5 Our God is full of peace and *love;*
    We on his word rely;
And still his tender mercies prove
    When to his arms we fly.

XLIII. *The Goodness of God.*

LET ev'ry tongue thy *goodness* speak,
    Thou sov'reign Lord of all!
Thy strength'ning hands uphold the weak,
    And raise the poor that fall.

2 When sorrows bow the spirit down,
 Or virtue lies distrest,
Beneath the proud oppressor's frown
 Thou giv'st the mourner rest.

3 The Lord supports our infant days,
 And guides our giddy youth:
Holy and just are all thy ways,
 And all thy works are truth.

4 Thou know'st the pains thy servants feel:
 Thou hear'st thy children's cry,
And their best wishes to fulfil,
 Thy grace is ever nigh.

5 Thy *mercy* never shall remove
 From men of hearts sincere:
Thou sav'st the souls whose humble lo
 Is join'd with holy fear.

6 My lips shall dwell upon thy praise,
 And spread thy fame abroad:
Let all the sons of Adam raise
 The honours of their God.

XLIV. *Affliction.*

THEE, Jesus, full of truth and peace;
 Thee, Saviour, we adore!
Thee, in *affliction's furnace* praise
 And magnify thy pow'r.

2 Thy pow'r, in human weakness shewn,
 Shall make us all entire:
We now thy guardian presence own,
 And walk unburnt in *fire*.

3 Thee

3 Thee, Son of man! by faith we see,
    And glory in our guide;
Surrounded and upheld by thee,
    The fiery test abide.

4 The fire our graces shall refine,
    Till moulded from above,
We bear the character divine,
    The stamp of perfect love.

XLV. *A Storm at Sea.*

₊ NOW floating waves and billows roar,
    And seas in mountains rise!
O God, thy mercy we implore,
    Regard our feeble cries!

2 The raging elements declare
    Our latest hour is come;
And ev'ry wave bids us prepare
    For our eternal home.

3 Far from the aid of human pow'r,
    No pilot here to save;
We're still expecting ev'ry hour
    The seas to prove our grave.

4 Now that our dangers still increase,
    Ah! whither can we flee?
In this the time of our distress,
    O Lord! but unto thee.

5 Descend in mercy from above,
    Compose the raging tide;
And let thy pow'r and goodness prove
    Our safe and only guide.

6 O God! in this diftrefsful hour,
    Thy aid we now implore ;
Conduct us by thy guardian pow'r,
    To our intended fhore.

XLVI. *The Shortnefs and Uncertainty of Life.*

THEE we adore, eternal name,
    And humbly own to thee,
How feeble is our mortal frame,
    What dying worms we be!

2 Our wafting lives grow fhorter ftill,
    As days and months increafe ;
And ev'ry beating pulfe we tell
    Leaves but the number lefs.

3 The year rolls round, and fteals away
    The breath that firft it gave :
Whate'er we do, where'er we be,
    We're trav'ling to the grave.

4 Dangers ftand thick thro' all the ground,
    To pufh us to the tomb ;
And fierce difeafes wait around,
    To hurry mortals home.

5 Infinite joy or endlefs woe
    Attend on ev'ry breath;
And yet, how unconcern'd we go,
    Upon the brink of death?

6 Waken, O Lord! our drowfy fenfe,
    To walk this dang'rous road :
And if our fouls be hurry'd hence,
    May they be found with God.

XLVII. *Evening.*

XLVII. *Evening.*

⁂ LORD let my *ev'ning* sacrifice,
    Ascend before thee to the skies;
      The praises of my tongue:
All glory, might, and majesty,
And pow'r divine, do unto thee
      Eternally belong.

2 This *day* thy mercy stood prepar'd,
My sure defence, and constant guard,
      From Satan's hellish pow'r;
Th' impending stroke thou didst avert,
Sustain'd my soul in ev'ry part
      Unto the present hour.

3 O that my soul could rightly serve,
The God who does my life preserve,
      And still from day to day,
Upholds me by his mighty pow'r,
While death stands waiting at the door
      To snatch my breath away.

4 Now that the curtain of the night
Precludes my eyes from nat'ral light,
      I'll give myself to sleep;
Assur'd that thou, in ev'ry hour,
Wilt still, secure from Satan's pow'r,
      My soul in safety keep.

XLVIII. *Scriptures.*

INSPIRER of the antient seers,
    Who wrote the sacred page;
Preserv'd thro' all succeeding years,
    To our degen'rate age.

2 While in thy word we search for thee,
   (We search with trembling awe!)
Open our eyes, and let us see
   The wonders of thy law.

3 Now let our darkness comprehend
   The light that shines so clear;
Now the revealing Spirit send,
   And give us ears to hear,

4 Before us let thy goodness pass,
   Which here by faith we know;
Let us, in Jesus, see thy face,
   And die to all below,

XLIX. *For King George.*

⁂ THOU King of nations, who ordain'st
   The pow'rs on earth that be!
By whom our lawful sov'reign reigns,
   Upheld by none but thee.

2 We now in faith and humble pray'r,
   For him, thy grace implore;
Make him the object of thy care,
   Both now and evermore.

3 As loyal subjects to his pow'r,
   We own his mild command;
Defend and guard him ev'ry hour
   By thine Almighty hand.

4 When his malignant foes invent,
   Or yet sedition spread;
O! let thine angels pitch their tent
   Around his sacred head.

5 From private and from open foes,
  Him constantly rescue;
And those that would his laws oppose,
  Lord! instantly subdue.

L. *The Love of God.*

MY God, for all I am and have,
  And all I hope to be,
Here, and beyond the closing grave,
  The praise I owe to thee.

2 But not a thousand hymns of praise,
  From such a tongue as mine,
Nor yet a song in seraph's lays,
  Can speak such *love* as thine.

3 Thy *love* in the Redeemer shewn,
  When given up to die;
The Father's best beloved Son,
  For sinners such as I.

4 That *love* which has the Spirit giv'n
  To bring the tidings near;
To put me in the way to heav'n,
  And safe conduct me there:

5 And ev'ry comfort of the way
  Thy lib'ral hand bestows;
Leads me to own from day to day
  The *love* from which it flows.

6 Dear God, assist my lab'ring tongue,
  While I attempt thy praise;
And fit me to pursue the song,
  Thro' everlasting days.

LI. *Heaven.*

LI. *Heaven.*

※ OUR sorrows and desponding fears,
    Are now at last o'ercome;
The new *Jerusalem* appears,
    Our everlasting home.

2 From earth and sin we now remove,
    To our divine abode;
The house of angel saints above,
    The palace of our God.

3 Our mourning days are at an end,
    And all our sorrows fled;
We now triumphantly ascend
    To Christ our living head.

4 Here dawns an everlasting day,
    Ne'er clouded by the night;
Here love and mercy still display,
    A permanent delight.

5 Here faithful saints obtain the grace,
    (Who knew their sins forgiv'n)
To see unveil'd the Prince of Peace,
    The Majesty of heav'n.

LII. *Servants.*

FORTH in the morning, Lord, I go,
    My *labour* to pursue;
Thee, only thee, resolv'd to know,
    In all I speak or do.

2 The task thy wisdom has assign'd,
    I'll chearfully fulfil:
In all my *works* thy presence find,
    And do thy blessed will.

3 Thy bright example I pursue;
    To thee in all things rise;
And all I think, or speak, or do,
    Is one great sacrifice.

4 Careless thro' outward toils I go,
    From all distraction free:
My *hands* are but engag'd below,
    My *heart* is still with thee.

LIII. *Masters.*

***MASTER supreme, to thee I cry
    For constant pow'r and grace;
Thy bright example still to eye,
    And all thy footsteps trace.

2 Make me a pattern to my house,
    That all beneath my care,
May studiously thy precepts chuse,
    And all thy goodness share.

3 To those that wait upon my call
    May I with love behave;
And daily think how soon we'll all
    Be equal in the grave.

4 Teach me to balance well my pow'r
    With due prudential care,
Lest I should ever chance to grow
    Remiss or too severe.

5 O'er him who frequent error makes
    I'll keep a watchful eye;
But unavoidable mistakes
    I'll heedlesly pass by.

LIV. *For Parents.*

COME, Father, Son, and Holy Ghost!
　　To whom we for our *children* cry;
The good desir'd and wanted most,
　　Out of thy richest grace supply,

2 Error and ignorance remove,
　　Their blindness both of heart and mind:
Give them the wisdom from above,
　　Spotless, and peaceable, and kind.

3 Learning's redundant part and vain,
　　Be here cut off and cast aside;
But let them, Lord, the substance gain,
　　In ev'ry solid truth abide.

4 Let them acquire and ne'er forego
　　The pious lessons to them giv'n;
The knowledge fit for man to know,
　　To train and bring them up for heav'n,

LV. *Youth.*

⁂ FATHER, to thee we lift our eyes,
　　For thee our hearts prepare;
Attend in mercy to our cries,
　　Regard our humble pray'r.

2 Thro' all our heedless steps in youth,
　　Yea ev'ry day and night,
Instruct, by thy unerring truth,
　　Our infant minds aright.

3 Whene'er we carelessly expose
　　Ourselves to Satan's snare;
O God! in mercy interpose,
　　Be thou assistant there.

4 O! let our conscience always be
  Imprest with filial awe;
And ope our eyes that we may see,
  The wonders of thy law.

LVI. *Mariners.*

THY works of glory, mighty Lord!
  Thy wonders in the *deeps!*
The sons of courage shall record,
  Who trade in floating *ships.*

2 At thy command the *winds* arise,
  And swell the tow'ring *waves;*
The *men* astonish'd mount the skies,
  And sink in yawning graves.

3 Again they climb the wat'ry hills,
  And plunge the deeps again;
Each like a tott'ring drunkard reels,
  And finds his courage vain.

4 Then to the Lord they raise their cries,
  He hears their loud request,
And orders silence thro' the skies,
  And lays the *floods* to *rest.*

5 'Tis God that brings them safe to land;
  Let *stupid mortals know,*
That *waves* are under his command,
  And all the *winds* that blow!

LVII. *Parents.*

GREAT *Parent* of the human race,
  Let us be taught by thee;
How we may train, in all thy ways,
  Our rising progeny.

2 Help us their passions to subdue,
    Whenever we reprove;
And by thy grace their minds renew,
    With wisdom from above.

3 Inspire us with parental care,
    As guardians of their youth,
That studiously we may prepare
    Their minds for virtuous truth.

4 We would induce them to obey;
    With gentleness proceed;
And never take the roughest way
    When love will do the deed.

5 T' accomplish this important task,
    Let grace to us be giv'n;
With ev'ry blessing that we ask,
    To train them up for heav'n.

LVIII. *Thanks after a Storm at Sea.*

THINK, O my soul! devoutly think,
    How with affrighted eyes,
Thou saw'st the wide extended deep
    In all its *horror* rise.

2 Confusion dwelt in ev'ry face,
    And fear in ev'ry heart;
When gulfs on gulfs, and waves on waves,
    O'ercame the pilot's art.

3 Yet then from all my griefs, O Lord!
    Thy mercy set me free;
Whilst in the confidence of pray'r
    My soul took hold on thee.

4 The storm was *laid*, the winds *retir'd*,
  Obedient to thy will;
The sea that roar'd at thy command,
  At thy command was still.

5 In midst of danger, fears, and death,
  Thy goodness I'll adore;
And praise thee for thy mercies past,
  And humbly hope for more.

6 My life, if thou preserv'st my life,
  Thy sacrifice shall be;
And death, when death shall be my doom,
  Shall join my soul to thee.

LIX. *Longing for Heaven.*

⁂ COME, quickly come, most gracious Lord!
  Fulfil the promise of thy word;
    And make me one with thee:
Enrol my name among the blest,
That in thy bosom I may rest
    To all eternity.

2 The tree of life I long to taste,
On which thy ransom'd servants feast,
    The fruit of love divine.
The chrystal streams beneath thy throne,
Of which the saints, and they alone,
    Can drink when they incline.

3 There I shall soon forget my fears,
When once above this vail of tears;
    By Jesus' side set down:
May I by faith this prize ensure,
And here with patience still endure
    The Cross to wear the Crown.

LX. *The Creation.*

THE spacious firmament on high,
   With all the blue æthereal sky,
And spangled heav'ns, (a shining frame)
Their great original proclaim.

2 Th' unweary'd sun from day to day
Doth his Creator's pow'r display;
And publishes to ev'ry land,
The work of an Almighty hand.

3 Soon as the ev'ning shades prevail,
The moon takes up the wond'rous tale;
And nightly to the list'ning earth
Repeats the story of her birth:

4 Whilst all the stars that round her burn,
And all the planets in their turn,
Confirm the tidings as they roll,
And spread the truth from pole to pole.

5 What tho' in solemn silence all
Move round the dark terrestrial ball?
What tho' no real voice nor sound
Amidst their radiant orbs be found?

6 In Reason's ear they all rejoice,
And utter forth a glorious voice,
Forever singing as they shine,
" The hand that made us is divine."

LXI. *Public Worship.*

⁎ ALMIGHTY God, we now appear
   Before thy throne of grace;
With fervent love and holy fear
   We seek thy gracious face.

2 Thy pard'ning mercy, Lord reveal
 To ev'ry waiting heart;
And ev'ry wounded spirit heal
 Before that we depart.

3 How often, Lord, have we appear'd
 Before thy face in vain?
How many precepts have we heard?
 Yet few do we retain.

4 In all thy glory now appear,
 And on our spirits shine;
And fill the souls that here attend
 With faith and love divine.

5 And those that now their sins lament,
 Who for their pardon wait;
O! may such mourning souls be sent
 Rejoicing from thy gate.

LXII. *Judgment.*

WHEN rising from the bed of death,
 O'erwhelm'd with guilt and fear,
I *see* my *Maker* face to face,
 O how shall I appear?

2 If yet, while pardon may be found,
 And mercy may be sought,
My heart with inward horror shrinks
 And trembles at the thought:

3 When thou, O Lord! shalt stand disclos'd
 In majesty severe,
And sit in *judgment* on my soul,
 O how shall I appear?

4 But

4 But thou haſt told the troubled mind,
    Who does her ſins lament,
The timely tribute of her tears,
    Shall endleſs woe prevent.

5 Then ſee the ſorrows of my heart,
    Ere yet it be too late;
And hear my Saviour's dying groans,
    To give thoſe ſorrows weight.

6 For never ſhall my ſoul deſpair
    Her pardon to procure,
Who knows thy only Son has dy'd
    To make her pardon ſure.

LXIII. *Glorification thro' Chriſt.*

⁎ BEHOLD what countleſs numbers ſtand
    In robes of white array'd;
With palms of vict'ry in their hand,
    And crowns upon their head.

2 Theſe ſaints to endleſs glory came,
    From great diſtreſs below,
And waſh'd their robes in blood divine,
    And made them white as ſnow.

3 They now the throne of God ſurround,
    Before Meſſiah fall;
In ſongs of praiſe their trumpets ſound
    To him that died for all.

4 Triumphing over death and ſin,
    They find their trials o'er;
And join in an exalted hymn,
    Their Saviour to adore.

LXIV. *Judgment.*

LO! he comes with clouds descending,
    Once for favour'd sinners slain,
Thousand, thousand saints attending,
    Swell the triumph of his train.
        Hallelujah!
    God appears on earth to reign.

2 Ev'ry eye shall now behold him,
    Rob'd in dreadful majesty;
Those that set at nought and fold him,
    Pierc'd and nail'd him to the tree,
        Deeply wailing,
    Shall the true Messiah see.

3 The dear tokens of his passion
    Still his dazzling body bears,
Cause of endless exultation
    To his ransom'd worshippers:
        With what rapture
    Gaze we on those glorious scars.

4 Yea, amen! let all adore thee,
    High on thine eternal throne;
Saviour, take the pow'r and glory,
    Claim the kingdom for thine own,
        Jah, Jehovah,
    Everlasting God, come down!

LXV. *Morning.*

⁂ THY praise, O God! I'll sound abroad,
    And still to sinners shew;
How sov'reign grace, in ev'ry place,
    Protects thy saints below.

2 Mine eyes survey the rising sky
    With pleasure and delight;
And waking find I call to mind
    The slumbers of the night.

3 Thee I adore, who didst restore
    My life and pow'rs to me!
Who, when asleep, didst safely keep
    My soul from danger free.

4 Tho' dangers roll around my soul,
    Yet still thy wakeful eyes,
And guardian pow'r, make me secure
    From all beneath the skies.

5 This day protect, and still direct
    My soul to follow thee;
Until that day, when thou shalt say,
    "Come hither up to me."

LXVI. *The Christian's Character.*

WHO shall inhabit in thy hill?
    O God of holiness!
Whom will the Lord admit to dwell
    So near his throne of grace?

2 The man that walks in pious ways,
    And works with righteous hands;
That trusts his Maker's promises,
    And follows his commands.

3 He speaks the meaning of his heart,
    Nor slanders with his tongue;
Will scarce believe an ill report,
    Nor do his neighbour wrong.

4 He always makes his promise good,
    Whatever loss he bears;
" Nor once revokes what he hath said,
    To change the word he swears."

5 His hands disdain a golden bribe,
    And never gripe the poor:
This man shall dwell with God on earth,
    And find his heav'n secure.

LXVII. *The Sufferings of Christ.*

⁎⁎ WHAT mortal can entirely scan
    The *sufferings* of our Head;
Which ev'ry hour he did endure,
    In guilty sinners stead.

2 In swaddling bands, to foreign lands,
    From Herod's sword he flies:
By Satan tried, and food deny'd,
    He fasted forty days.

3 He was despis'd, and stigmatiz'd,
    Where he himself was born;
Was false accus'd, and basely us'd,
    With insolence and scorn.

4 Birds of the air could nests prepare,
    And safe retirement had;
But Christ possest no place of rest
    Whereon to lay his head.

5 If forth he threw th' infernal crew,
    To health the sick restor'd;
In league combin'd, with Satan join'd,
    They charge our blessed Lord.

6 All

6 All these and more, he mildly bore,
   To ransom thee and me;
At last did die, that he might buy
   Our pardon on the tree.

LXVIII. *The C. Psalm.*

BEFORE Jehovah's awful throne,
   Ye nations bow with sacred joy:
Know that the Lord is God alone;
   He can create, and he destroy.

2 His sov'reign pow'r without our aid,
   Made us of clay, and form'd us men:
And when like wand'ring sheep we stray'd,
   He brought us to his fold again.

3 We'll croud thy gates with thankful songs,
   High as the heav'ns our voices raise;
And earth with her ten thousand tongues,
   Shall fill thy courts with sounding praise.

4 Wide as the world is thy command;
   Vast as eternity thy love;
Firm as a rock thy truth must stand,
   When rolling years shall cease to move.

LXIX. *Evening.*

*** WASTING days are rolling on;
   We are hast'ning to our home;
Time consumes the day at last,
None regains the one that's past.
We no more this day enjoy;
How we did the same employ?
God may now at us enquire,
Cite us to his bar severe.

2 Now

2 Now before we close our eyes,
Can we in the Lord rejoice?
Do we know that sov'reign grace
Guards our souls in ev'ry place?
Saviour now these gifts impart,
Write such blessings on our heart:
That we still at peace may be,
With our minds, the world, and thee:

3 When our beds shall prove our grave,
Then our souls from Satan save;
When we from the grave arise,
May we meet thee in the skies:
Still to that important hour,
Guide us by thy mighty pow'r;
In the darkness be our light,
Guard us thro' the shades of night.

LXX. *Preservation thro' Christ.*

TO Heav'n I lift my waiting eyes,
    Where all my hopes are laid;
The Lord, who built the earth and skies,
    Is my perpetual aid.

2 Their feet shall never slide nor fall,
    Whom he designs to keep;
His ear attends the softest call;
    His eyes can never sleep.

3 He will sustain our weakest pow'rs
    With his Almighty arm,
And watch our most unguarded hours
    Against surprising harm.

4 Rejoice

4 Rejoice ye saints, and rest secure,
    Your keeper is the Lord;
His watchful eyes employ his pow'r
    For your eternal guard.

5 No scorching sun, nor sickly moon,
    Shall have his leave to smite;
He shields our head from burning noon,
    Or blasting damps by night.

6 He guards our souls, he keeps our breath,
    Where thickest dangers come:
Go and return, secure from death,
    Till Christ command us home.

LXXI. *Intercession of Christ.*

*** BEFORE the throne our Surety stands,
    His wounds are open'd wide;
For us he spreads his bleeding hands,
    And shews his open side.

2 Our service at the throne of grace
    Would ineffectual prove,
If Jesus did not *intercede*,
    And plead his dying love.

3 Altho' on the expiring tree
    The ransom was laid down;
Still Jesus *pleads* for thee and me,
    Till we obtain the crown.

4 Thro' Jesus' death we are redeem'd
    By price, as well as pow'r;
He *pleads* for us, and still applies
    His merit ev'ry hour.

5 Redemption by his Spirit's pow'r,
   Unto a sinner's giv'n;
When soul and body are renew'd,
   And both made meet for heav'n.

LXXII. *Sickness.*

1 *O* God! before thy mercy-seat,
   I now present my cry;
If thou withdraw'st, or hid'st thy face,
   Ah! whither can I fly?

2 Remember undeserved love;
   Thy pity I implore;
In mercy my physician prove,
   My former *health* restore.

3 My plaintive sighs, and daily groans,
   Are sounding in thine ears;
Thy watchful eye does still behold,
   And numbers all my tears.

4 Upon a bed of sickness laid,
   Beneath affliction prest;
Still ev'ry day and ev'ry hour,
   I'm panting after rest.

5 Thou great Physician of my soul,
   In mercy now draw nigh;
My *weak diseased* body heal,
   And save me, or I die.

LXXIII. *Thanks after Sickness.*

O Thou! who, when I did complain,
   Didst all my griefs remove;
Saviour, do not now disdain
   My humble praise and love.

2 Since thou a pitying ear didst give,
  And heard me when I pray'd,
I'll call upon thee while I live,
  And never doubt thy aid.

3 Pale death, with all his ghastly train,
  My soul *encompas'd round:*
Anguish, and sin, and dread, and pain,
  On ev'ry side I found

4 To thee, O Lord of life! I pray'd,
  And did for succour flee;
O! save (in my distress I said)
  The soul that trusts in thee.

5 How good thou art! how large thy grace,
  How easy to forgive!
The helpless thou delight'st to raise;
  And by thy love I live.

6 Then O, my soul! be never more
  With anxious thoughts distrest:
God's bount'ous love doth thee restore
  To ease, and joy, and rest.

7 My eyes no longer drown'd with tears,
  My feet from falling free;
Redeem'd from death and guilty fears,
  O Lord! I'll live to thee.

LXXIV. *Evening.*

⁂ MY God, to thee I lift my eyes,
  Thy goodness I admire;
That I, supported by thy grace,
  Have seen this day expire.

2 Thro'

2 Thro' each unguarded scene of life,
    Thy mercy stood prepar'd:
Thy mighty pow'r I still have found
    My sure and stedfast guard.

3 Now let me *rest* my weary head,
    From death and danger free!
And all my waking thoughts engage
    Betwixt my soul and thee.

4 My life to thy protecting pow'r,
    I'll chearfully resign;
With my immortal spirit too,
    For both, O Lord! are thine.

5 Reviving slumbers me afford,
    My wasted strength renew;
That in the morning I may rise
    Thy glory to pursue.

LXXV. *The Holiness of God.*

SHALL the vile race of flesh and blood
Contend with their Creator, God?
Shall mortal worms presume to be
More holy, wise, or just, than he?

2 Behold he puts his trust in none
Of all the Spirits round his throne;
Their natures, when compar'd with his,
Are neither holy, just, nor wise.

3 But how much meaner things are they
Who spring from dust, and dwell in clay.
Touch'd by the finger of thy wrath,
We faint and perish like the moth.

4 Almighty Lord, to thee we bow:
How *sinful* we, how *holy* thou!
No more the sons of earth shall dare
With an eternal God compare.

LXXVI. *Humility.*

⁂ WITH meekness and humility,
  Array my soul within;
This mantle best becometh me,
  An heir of death and sin.

2 Are angels *meek?* shall man be *proud?*
  May I the thought detest!
O let this vice ne'er be allow'd,
  Within my mind to rest.

3 How vain for mortal man to trust
  In gold, or shining forms!
Who soon must mingle with the dust,
  A feast for reptile worms.

4 For all the gifts we here enjoy,
  Are lent us to improve,
Nor can we rightly them employ
  Unaided from above.

5 For those whom heaven favours most,
  That an abundance have,
Have cause to thank, but not to boast,
  For all that they receive.

LXXVII. *The Resurrection of Christ.*

⁂ WHEN I the sacred tomb behold,
  Where my Redeemer lay;
I see fulfill'd what prophets told,
  And death and hell defy.

2 Our Jesus, now high thron'd above,
   Resign'd his vital breath;
But yet the empty grave does prove
   His conquest over death.

3 My risen Saviour I behold,
   Once number'd with the dead;
But now upon a throne of gold,
   My prophet, priest, and head.

4 Since Christ has vanquish'd death and hell,
   As my Almighty head;
He will not leave my flesh to dwell
   For ever with the dead.

5 Now in the dust my mortal frame,
   I chearfully can leave;
'Tis but a while it can remain
   A tenant of the grave.

LXXVIII. *Old Age.*

BENEATH a load of cares and years,
   Lo! *age* begins to bend;
The lamp of life but weakly flames,
   When drawing near its end.

2 Now dim all round the prospect shows
   To his short-sighted eye,
While ev'ry former pleasure fades
   And perishes away.

3 Wave after wave has beat so long,
   Just o'er his *hoary head;*
That in the furrows of the brow,
   His sorrows you may read.

4 The dregs of being now he tastes,
 And drags the load of life,
Oft calling for the grisly King,
 To end the tedious strife.

5 Think, *ye* that stoop towards the tomb,
 This life draws near an end,
Soon must you bid this world adieu,
 Your course to others bend.

LXXIX. *Redemption thro' Christ.*

MY wasting days shall sound thy praise,
 Thou dear redeeming Lord,
Thy life for mine, thou didst resign,
 And me to health restor'd.

2 The wrath of God, a weighty load!
 Was resting on my head;
But Jesus gave himself to *save*,
 And *suffer'd* in my stead.

3 His blood was shed in sinners stead,
 And speaks them now *forgiv'n*;
Thro' Christ our head, we now can read
 Our title clear for heav'n.

4 While here below, we'll daily shew,
 Our love and praise to thee,
Who hast by grace, procur'd our peace,
 And pardon on the tree.

5 When we remove to heav'n above,
 And in full glory shine,
There we'll adore, for evermore,
 That matchless love of thine.

LXXX. *Youth.*

LXXX. *Youth.*

YE thoughtless tribes, whose glowing cheek,
   Youth paints with rosy hue;
Think how the rusty hand of time
   Will wrinkle soon your brow.

2 Now joy beats high in ev'ry pulse,
   Health sparkles in your eye,
Each morn in quest of new delight;
   In sanguine mood you fly.

3 But mind that pleasure's cup will sour,
   And sweetest joys grow stale;
Thy ear regardless soon will hear
   Life's antiquated tale.

4 O! catch the golden youthful days,
   While stretching on the wing;
These, when deep furrows plow the cheek,
   Will richest cordials bring.

5 While *youthful* warmth inspires the heart,
   To him its throne resign,
Who with these sparkling beams of hope,
   Has made thy brow to shine.

6 By impulse of supernal grace,
   Still turn thy soul to God,
For that magnetic virtue seek,
   Which points to his abode.

LXXXI. *Heaven.*

*** OUR doubting fears, and flowing tears,
   For ever now be gone;
We thro' the sky ascend on high,
   To our eternal *home.*

2 By Christ our Lord to life restor'd,
    And everlasting bliss;
We now prepare his love to share,
    Of endless happiness.

3 Jesus our guide, shall still abide,
    His blessings to impart;
His love and peace, shall still increase
    In our believing heart.

4 We now shall taste that blessed feast,
    The fruit of love divine;
And daily stand at God's right hand,
    And in his presence shine.

5 With heart and voice let us rejoice,
    Our Advocate we see:
His praise around, with trumpets sound,
    To all eternity.

LXXXII. *The Resurrection of Christ.*

THE Sun of Righteousness appears,
    To set in blood no more:
Adore the scatt'rer of your fears;
    Your *rising* Sun adore!

2 The saints, when he resign'd his breath,
    Unclos'd their sleeping eyes:
He breaks again the bands of death,
    Again the dead arise.

3 Alone the dreadful race he ran,
    Alone the wine-press trode,
He dy'd and suffer'd as a man,
    But *rises* as a God.

4 In vain the stone, the watch, the seal,
    Forbid an early rise;
To him who breaks the gates of hell,
    And opens Paradise.

LXXXIII. *Judgment.*

_{*} JEHOVAH sends a herald forth,
    His sov'reign will to spread;
Whose trumpet sounds from south to north,
    And wakes the sleeping dead.

2 Attending seraphs thro' the sky
    Proclaim th' approaching God;
And vainly guilty sinners fly,
    His sin-avenging rod.

3 The flinty rock its aid denies,
    The sinner's grief to share;
While the arch-angel's trumpet cries,
    " To meet your God prepare."

4 The rising dead approaching near,
    Desert the empty tomb;
In dread suspence they wait to hear,
    Their last decisive doom.

5 When earth, and sea, and sun, and moon,
    Before thy presence flee;
When thou for judgment dost come down,
    O Lord, remember me!

LXXXIV. *The Resurrection of Christ.*

CHRIST from the dead is *rais'd*, and made
    The first fruits of the tomb;
For as by man came death, by man
    Did Resurrection come.

2 For as from Adam, all mankind
    Did guilt and death derive,
So, by the righteousness of Christ,
    Shall all be made alive.

3 If then ye risen are with Christ,
    Seek only how to get
The things which are above, where Christ
    At God's right hand is set.

LXXXV. *The Goodness of God.*

⁎⁎⁎ TO praise the Lord, with one accord,
    Let all our pow'rs agree:
In rapture sing, to God our King,
    Who form'd both earth and sea.

2 To God on high, who rules the sky,
    And all the starry frame;
Let praises flow from all below,
    To his Almighty name.

3 He on his wings salvation brings,
    To ev'ry humble heart;
And life, and peace, with saving grace,
    He doth to them impart.

4 Thou'lt daily *grant*, whate'er we want,
    And nought that's *good* deny;
For none shall be forgot by thee,
    That on thy *grace* rely.

5. Thy *goodness*, Lord, is still ador'd
    By saints in earth and heav'n;
May we outshine, in praise divine,
    Whose debt of sin's forgiv'n.

LXXXVI. *The Incarnation of Christ.*

COME, thou long expected Jesus!
  Born to set thy people free;
From our fears and sins release us,
  Let us find our rest in thee.

2 Israel's strength and consolation,
  Hope of all the earth thou art;
Dear desire of ev'ry nation,
  Joy of ev'ry longing heart.

3 *Born* thy people to deliver,
  Born a child and yet a King,
Born to reign in us for ever,
  Now thy gracious kingdom bring.

By thine own eternal Spirit,
  Rule in all our hearts alone;
By thine all-sufficient merit,
  Raise us to thy glorious throne.

LXXXVII. *Humility and Contentment.*

IN riches never make thy boast,
  Nor glory in thy might;
Nor yet in mortal honours trust,
  That take a rapid flight.

2 The rusty hand of time impairs
  The warlike strength of man;
And they that move in highest spheres,
  Their days are but a span.

3 The riches, gold, and hoarded wealth,
  Acquir'd by fraud and strife;
Can never once preserve our health,
  Nor yet protract our life.

4 The

4 The proud, aspiring empty fool,
    How vain is all his trust,
When groaning in affliction's school,
    Or blended with the dust.

5 See how each object round our eyes
    Does giddy mortals shew,
That lasting comforts seldom rise
    From happiness below.

LXXXVIII. *Public Worship.*

JESUS, thou all redeeming Lord!
    Thy blessing we implore,
Open the door to preach thy word,
    The great effectual door.

2 Gather the outcasts in, and save
    From sin and Satan's pow'r!
And let them now salvation have,
    And know their gracious hour.

3 Lover of souls, thou know'st to prize
    What thou hast bought so dear;
Come now, and in thy people's eyes,
    With all thy wounds appear!

4 Appear, as when of old confest
    The suff'ring Son of God;
And let them see thee in thy vest
    But newly dipt in blood.

5 Thy feet were nail'd to yonder tree,
    To trample down their sin;
Thy hands they all stretch'd out may see,
    To take thy murd'rers in.

6 Thy side an open fountain is,
    Where all may freely go,
And drink the living streams of bliss,
    And wash them white as snow.

7 Ready thou art the blood t' apply
    And prove the record true;
And all thy wounds to sinners cry,
    " I suffer'd this for YOU!"

LXXXIX. *Justification by Faith.*

⁎⁎ IN fruitless toil the sons of men,
    Their legal schemes devise:
A Christless law will still condemn,
    'Tis *faith* that justifies.

2 The law, upon the slightest fault,
    Condemns us to our face;
But *faith* to penitents declare,
    Their Jesus' pard'ning grace.

3 If Moses' laws sufficient were,
    Our sins to justify;
For whom did Jesus live, and weep,
    And pray, and bleed, and die?

4 'Tis only *faith* in Jesus' blood,
    That can our guilt remove;
But let this faith be always such
    As works by fervent love.

5 When *faith* and *love* together join,
    They speak our sins forgiv'n;
Assisted by these cords divine,
    We scale the walls of heav'n.

XC. *Faith in Christ.*

LOVERS of pleasure more than God,
    For you he suffer'd pain:
Swearers, for you he spilt his blood;
    And shall he bleed in vain?

2 Misers, his life for you he paid,
    Your basest crime he bore:
Drunkards, your sins on him were laid,
    That you might sin no more.

3 The God of love to earth he came,
    That you might come to heav'n;
Believe, believe in Jesus' name,
    And all your sin's forgiv'n!

4 Believe in him that dy'd for thee;
    And sure as he hath dy'd,
Thy debt is paid, thy soul is free,
    And thou art justify'd.

XCI. *Preservation thro' Christ.*

*** I WILL not fear, while Christ is near,
    The pow'rs of death and hell;
Thro' him I shall subdue them all,
    Their mighty force repel.

2 I've always found his pow'r around.
    My soul on ev'ry side,
In doubts and fears, he still appears
    My sure and constant guide.

3 His mighty pow'r, does ev'ry hour
    Sustain my feeble mind;
In boundless love, I daily prove
    Him merciful and kind.

4 His endless praise, my soul shall raise
  While in this house of clay;
And when I stand at his right hand,
  Where sin is done away:

5 Then shall I join with saints divine,
  His glory to adore,
And ever see the One in three,
  When time shall be no more.

XCII. *Hell.*

TERRIBLE thought! shall I alone,
  Who may be sav'd, shall I
Of all, alas! whom I have known,
  Thro' sin for ever die?

2 While all my old companions dear,
  With whom I once did live,
Joyful at God's right hand appear,
  A blessing to receive?

3 Shall I, amidst a ghastly band,
  Dragg'd to the judgment-seat,
Far on the left with horror stand,
  My fearful doom to meet?

4 While they enjoy his heav'nly love,
  Must I in torment dwell?
And howl, (while they sing hymns above)
  And blow the flames of *hell*.

5 Ah, no! I still may turn and live;
  For still his wrath delays;
He now vouchsafes a kind reprieve,
  And offers me his grace.

6 I will

6 I will accept his offers now,
 From ev'ry sin depart;
Perform my oft repeated vow,
 And render him my heart.

7 I will improve what I receive,
 The grace thro' Jesus giv'n;
Sure, if with God on earth I live,
 To live with God in heav'n.

XCIII. *Death.*

*** O DEATH! unnumber'd are thy slain,
 Resistless is thy pow'r,
Witness ye thousands that lie dead,
 Or gasping ev'ry hour.

2 Thy wide extended empire goes
 As far as life is spread;
And in thy chambers high and low,
 Must make their final bed.

3 O cruel unrelenting Death!
 Can none evade thy blow?
Must all resign their vital breath
 To thee their latest foe?

4 While musing o'er this fatal scene,
 My soul with horror cries,
" O Jesus! save me from the death,
 That never, never dies."

5 When death my life approaches nigh,
 And does his warrant bring;
My chiefest wish, is that he come
 Disarmed of his sting.

XCIV. *The*

XCIV. *The Power and Holiness of God.*

HOLY as thee, O Lord, is none!
Thy holiness is all thine own;
A drop of that unbounded sea
Is our's, a drop deriv'd from thee.

2 And when thy purity we share,
Thy only glory we declare,
And humbled into nothing own,
Holy and pure is God alone.

3 Sole self-existing God and Lord,
By all thy heav'nly hosts ador'd,
Let all on earth bow down to thee,
And own thy peerless Majesty:

4 That pow'r unparallel'd confess,
Establish'd on the rock of peace;
The rock that never shall remove,
The rock of pure Almighty love.

XCV. " *It is finished.*" John xix. 30.

THE fiery contest now is o'er,
The law receives its due;
If justice yet can ask for more,
My suff'rings I'll renew.

2 E'er I dismiss my soul and breath,
Let hell and wrath declare,
If ought remains for me on earth,
Of punishment to share.

3 Beneath the stroke of wrath and sin,
I now for sinners go;
But if defective, yet begin
And double ev'ry blow.

F 3.   4 I will

4 I will not yield my dying breath,
  Nor have my suit deny'd;
Nor enter thro' the gates of death,
  Till man is justify'd.

5 " 'Tis done," I know the ransom's paid,
  Father to thee I fly;
I now with pleasure bow my head,
  Dismiss my soul, and die.

XCVI. *Creation and Providence.*

ETERNAL Wisdom, thee we praise,
  Thee, the *creation* sings:
With thy loud name, rocks, hills, and seas,
  And heav'n's high palace rings.

2 Thy hand how wide it spreads the sky;
  How glorious to behold!
Ting'd with a blue of heav'nly dye,
  And starr'd with sparkling gold.

3 There thou hast bid the globes of light
  Their endless circles run:
There the pale planet rules the night:
  The day obeys the sun.

4 If down I turn my wand'ring eyes,
  On clouds and storms below:
Those under regions of the skies
  Thy num'rous glories shew.

5 The noisy winds stand ready there
  Thy wonders to obey:
With sounding wings they sweep the air,
  To make thy chariot way.

6 There like a trumpet, loud and strong,
    Thy thunder shakes our coast;
While the red lightnings wave along
    The banners of thy host.

7 On the thin air without a prop,
    Hang fruitful show'rs around:
At thy command they sink and drop,
    Their fatness on the ground.

8 Lo! here thy wond'rous skill arrays
    The earth in cheerful green!
A thousand herbs thy art displays,
    A thousand flow'rs between.

9 There, the rough mountains of the deep
    Obey thy strong command:
Thy breath can raise the billows steep,
    Or sink them to the sand.

10 Thy glories blaze all nature round,
    And strike the wond'ring sight,
Thro' skies, and seas, and solid ground,
    With terror and delight.

11 Infinite strength and equal skill,
    Shine thro' thy works abroad,
Our souls with vast amazement fill
    And speak the builder God.

12 But the mild glories of thy grace
    Our softer passions move:
Pity divine in Jesus' face,
    We see, adore, and love.

XCVII. *Preservation thro' Christ.*

*⁎*IN ev'ry hour, O God! thy pow'r
　　And providence I see;
While mortal death, in ev'ry breath,
　　Is warded off by thee.

2 I've all my days, beheld my ways
　　Sustain'd by sov'reign grace,
My faithful guide, on ev'ry side,
　　In ev'ry time and place.

3 Tho' dangers fly, I'll still defy
　　Their pow'r, and rapid tide;
Yea, sin and hell I'll both repel,
　　With *Jesus* by my side.

4 'Tis grace alone has ever done
　　Such mighty works for me;
For all my strength proves vain at length,
　　Unaided, Lord by thee.

5 I'll still disdain all earthly gain,
　　And pomp of human pride;
And nothing know on earth below,
　　But Jesus cruci'y'd.

XCVIII. *The Life of Christ.*

*⁎*WHILE our Redeemer here abode,
　　With flesh and blood below;
His unabated study was,
　　To lessen human woe.

2 T' avert affliction's falling stroke,
　　Or mitigate distress,
He always scatter'd where he went,
　　The seeds of happiness.

3. Whoever

3 Whoever did for aid apply,
  Deprest with grief or fear;
To them in mercy Jesus lent
  A sympathetic ear.

4 To numbers that could not discern
  The noon-day from the night,
His still successful healing hand
  Restor'd the pow'r of sight.

5 The tongues to silence long innur'd,
  Enabled were to talk:
The halt and lame he also cur'd,
  That both with ease might walk.

6 The sick and deaf, the wither'd limbs,
  Are heal'd at his command,
Dislodged demons, frighted, dread
  The vengeance of his hand.

XCIX. *The Attributes of God.*

O GOD, thou bottomless abyss!
  Thee to perfection who can know?
O height immense! what words suffice
  Thy countless *attributes* to shew?

2 Unfathomable depths thou art!
  O plunge me in thy mercy's sea;
Void of true wisdom is my heart,
  With love embrace and cover me!

3 While thee, all infinite I set
  By faith, before my ravish'd eye;
My weakness bends beneath the weight,
  O'erpow'r'd I sink, I faint, I die.

4 Eternity

4 Eternity thy fountain was,
  Which, like thee, no beginning knew;
Thou waſt, ere time began his race,
  Ere glow'd with ſtars th' ethereal blue.

5 Greatneſs unſpeakable is thine,
  Greatneſs, whoſe undiminiſh'd ray,
When ſhort-liv'd worlds are loſt, ſhall ſhine
  When earth and heav'n are fled away.

6 Unchangeable, all perfect Lord,
  Eſſential life's unbounded ſea;
What lives and moves, lives by thy word,
  It lives, and moves, and is from thee.

7 Thy parent-hand, thy forming ſkill,
  Firm fix'd this univerſal chain,
Elſe barren, empty, darkneſs ſtill
  Had held his unmoleſted reign:

8 Whate'er in earth, or ſea, or ſky,
  Or ſhuns or meets the wand'ring thought,
Eſcapes or ſtrikes the ſearching eye,
  By thee was to perfection brought.

9 High is thy pow'r above all height,
  Whate'er thy will decrees is done;
Thy wiſdom, equal to thy might,
  Only to thee, O God is known!

10 Heav'n's glory is thy awful throne,
  Yet earth partakes thy gracious ſway:
Vain man! thy wiſdom folly own,
  Loſt in thy reaſon's feeble ray:

11 What

11 What our dim eye could never see,
  Is plain and naked to thy sight,
What thickest darkness veils, to thee
  Shines clearly as the morning-light:

12 In light thou dwell'st; light, that no shade,
  No variation ever knew;
And heav'n and hell stand all display'd,
  And open to thy piercing view.

C. *A Soliloquy.*

⁂ I FEEL the healthy springs of life,
  My youthful mind inspire;
And softly whisper in my ear,
  " Fulfil thy heart's desire."

2 But unbrib'd conscience still declares;
  " Uncertain is thy breath,
Ere long thy health, thy strength, thy youth,
  Must all resign to death."

3 Can I my life or soul retain
  Within this house of clay,
When death in all his terror comes,
  To snatch them both away.

4 Ah, no! my ling'ring soul one day,
  Shall with reluctance leave
This tenement of dust—whilst it †
  Shall moulder in the grave.

5 What madness then for me to run,
  The mortal race of sin,
For which when temp'ral death is o'er,
  Eternal must begin!

† The Body.

CI. *Death.*

CI. *Death.*

⁂ GREAT God, at whose supreme command,
    My beating pulse began;
Unaided by thy mighty hand,
    How weak is mortal man?

2 How swiftly runs the ebbing sand,
    From life's uncertain glass,
And still impairs on ev'ry hand,
    As rolling years increase.

3 Dangers unknown in ambush lie,
    Where'er I stand or go;
And pain or sickness ev'ry day
    Attend my life below.

4 My soul and body, life and breath,
    By one unerring dart,
Shot from the iron hands of death,
    Must soon asunder part.

5 I know, I feel, I'm born to die,
    I view th' approaching hour,
When I must suddenly comply
    With death's destructive pow'r.

6 In distant worlds for me remains,
    What I cannot explore,
Eternal joy, or endless pains,
    When time shall be no more.

CII. *Public Worship.*

THOU Son of God, whose flaming eyes
    Our inmost thoughts perceive,
Accept the evening sacrifice,
    Which now to thee we give.

2 Is here a soul that knows thee not,
    Nor feels his want of thee?
A stranger to the blood that bought
    His pardon on the tree.

3 Convince him now of unbelief,
    His desp'rate state explain:
And fill his heart with sacred grief
    And penitential pain.

4 Speak with that voice that wakes the dead,
    And bid the sleeper rise,
And bid his guilty conscience dread,
    The death that never dies.

5 Extort the cry, what must be done
    To save a wretch like me?
How shall a trembling sinner shun
    That endless misery?

6 I must for faith incessant cry,
    And wrestle, Lord, with thee:
I must be born again, or die
    To all eternity.

CIII. "*O that they were Wise,*" &c. Deut. xxii. 29.

O! HOW ought mortal man to live,
    For God in all his ways,
While God bestows a kind reprieve,
    To lengthen out his days?

2 His constant wish, his daily care,
    While in this vail of tears,
Should be to watch, and still prepare
    Before that death appears.

3 Yet vain unthinking mortals here,
    Conclude that all is well;
And nothing dread nor nothing fear,
    While dropping into hell.

4 But O! if man would reason just
    (Of all beneath the skies)
On what can he repose his trust
    Wherein salvation lies?

5 Thy word, O God! and it alone,
    Can happiness secure;
When heav'n and earth are fled and gone,
    This pleasure will endure.

CIV. *The Attributes of God.*

HAIL, Father, Son, and Holy Ghost,
    One God in persons three;
Of thee we make our joyful boast,
    Our songs we make of thee.

2 Thou neither canst be felt nor seen,
    Thou art a *Spirit* pure;
Thou from *eternity* hast been,
    And *always* shalt endure.

3 *Present* alike in ev'ry place,
    Thy God-head we adore;
Beyond the bounds of time and space
    Thou dwell'st for evermore.

4 In *wisdom* infinite thou art,
    Thine eye doth all things see,
And ev'ry thought of ev'ry heart
    Is fully *known* to thee.

                            5 Whate'er

5 Whate'er thou wilt on earth below,
    Thou *doſt* in heav'n above:
But chiefly we rejoice to know
    Th' Almighty God of love.

6 Thou *lov'ſt* whate'er thy hands have made,
    Thy *goodneſs* we rehearſe,
In ſhining characters diſplay'd
    Throughout our univerſe.

CV. *The Sufferings of Chriſt.*

*** JESUS in our behalf has died:
    Behold ſuch boundleſs love!
Which, tho' with pain and anguiſh tried,
    No torment could remove.

2 O'erwhelming ſorrows as a flood,
    Into his ſoul were pour'd;
Yet firm his reſolution ſtood,
    And all the wrath endur'd.

3 Who can deſcribe the ardent love
    With which he took the cup!
What tongue can tell the pains of hell
    He felt to drink it up!

4 Behold th' amazing height of love!
    He prays and interceeds,
For thoſe who did his murd'rers prove
    His laſt petition pleads.

5 Both men and devils' cruel rage,
    He patiently ſuſtain'd;
And, when he trod the bloody ſtage,
    He never once complain'd.

6 When death at last did him release;
  The cords of life unty'd,
" 'Tis finish'd," cries the Prince of Peace,
  And bow'd his head, and died.

CVI. *The Eternity of God.*

THOU didst, O mighty God, exist
  Ere time began its race,
Before the ample elements
  Fill'd up the voids of space.

2 Before the pond'rous earthly globe
  On fluid air was stay'd:
Before the oceans mighty springs
  Their liquid stores display'd:

3 Ere thro' the gloom of ancient night
  The streaks of light appear'd:
Before the high celestial arch,
  Or starry poles were rear'd:

4 Before the loud melodious spheres
  Their tuneful round begun:
Before the shining roads of heav'n
  Were measur'd by the sun:

5 Ere men ador'd, or angels knew,
  Or prais'd thy wond'rous name:
Thy bliss (O! sacred spring of life)
  And glory were the same.

6 And when the pillars of the world
  With sudden ruin break,
And all the vast and goodly frame
  Sinks in the mighty wreck:

7 For

7 For ever permanent and fix'd,
    From agitation free,
Unchang'd in everlasting years
    Shall thy existence be.

CVII. *Death and Eternity.*

AN awful thought I call to mind,
    My last, my dying breath,
Where shall my soul a shelter find,
    Dislodg'd at last by *death?*

2 When anxious to retain her place,
    With death disputes the ground,
Shall she be banish'd from thy face,
    Or with the blest be found?

3 Celestial joys, or hellish pains,
    Reward my steps below;
There's no alternative remains,
    But happiness or woe.

4 Alarm'd by this, my spirit stands
    Convuls'd with grief and fear;
While I behold my ebbing-sands,
    And death approaching near.

5 While death suspends the fatal dart,
    And I thy grace enjoy;
How I may choose the better part,
    Let all my thoughts employ.

CVIII. *Judgment.*

YE virgin souls arise,
    With all the dead awake!
Unto salvation wise,
    Oil in your vessels take:

Upstarting at the midnight cry,
Behold the heav'nly bridegroom nigh.

2 He comes, he comes to call
   The nations to his bar,
   And raise to glory all
   Who meet for glory are;
Made ready for your full reward,
Go forth with joy to meet your Lord.

3 Go meet him in the sky,
   Your everlasting friend;
   Your Head to glorify,
   With all the saints ascend:
Ye pure in heart obtain the grace
To see without a veil his face.

4 Ye that have here receiv'd
   The unction from above
   And in his Spirit liv'd,
   Obedient to his love;
Jesus shall claim you for his bride:
Rejoice with all the sanctify'd!

5 The everlasting doors,
   Shall soon the saints receive,
   Above yon angel pow'rs
   In glorious joy to live;
Far from a world of grief and sin,
With God eternally shut in.

6 Then let us wait to hear
   The trumpet's welcome sound;
   To see our Lord appear,
   Watching let us be found;

When Jesus doth the heav'ns bow,—
Be found—as, Lord, thou find'st us now!

CIX. *Affliction.*

⁂ MY soul, shake off thy gloomy fears,
    With joy lift up thy voice;
'Tis Christ alone that wipes thy tears,
    And makes thee to rejoice.

2 No more thy trust nor courage yield
    When Satan's darts appear;
Jesus is thine Almighty shield,
    What then hast thou to fear?

3 Tho' clouds of darkness veil my mind,
    Yet these perplex in vain;
For Jesus' love I daily find,
    Revives my joys again.

4 My God's reviving grace can cheer,
    With light the gloomy cell,
And heav'n itself, if he's not there,
    Would soon be turn'd to hell.

5 'Tis but a few revolving years,
    When all our sorrows cease,
When God shall dry up all our tears,
    In everlasting peace.

CX. *The Gospel Trumpet.*

HARK how the gospel trumpets sound!
    Thro' all the earth they echo round;
For Jesus, by redeeming blood,
Is bringing sinners back to God,
And guides them safely by his word,
    To endless day.

2 Hail, all victorious conqu'ring Lord!
Be thou by all thy works ador'd,
 Who undertook for sinful man,
 And brought salvation thro' thy name,
 That we with thee might ever reign,
  In endless day.

3 Fight on ye conqu'ring souls, fight on;
And when the conquest ye have won,
 Then palms of vict'ry you shall bear,
 And in his kingdom have a share,
 Where crowns of glory ye shall wear;
  To endless day.

4 There we shall in sweet chorus join;
Where saints and angels all combine
 To sing of his redeeming love,
 When rolling years shall cease to move,
 And this shall be our theme above,
  In endless day.

CXI. *The Crucifixion of Christ.*

*** BY faith erect before your eyes
 Your Saviour, on the tree;
Behold him as a sacrifice,
 To set his people free.

2 Behold th' eternal Son of God
 Expos'd to open view,
Beneath affliction's cruel rod,
 By yon abandon'd crew.

3 Reproach and shame he mildly bore,
 From earth and hell combin'd:
How was his spotless Spirit tore
 With griefs of ev'ry kind?

4 What

4 What an amazing sight is this,
    Which on the cross we see?
Shall Christ who never did amiss,
    To death devoted be?

5 Behold and see the Saviour's grace:
    He voluntarly flies
From heav'n above—assumes our place,
    And for our sins he dies.

6 No human ransom could release
    Our souls from Satan's pow'r;
But Jesus did make up our peace,
    In that important hour.

CXII. *A Prayer for the Church.*

JESUS, may thy true members shine
    Illustrious as the sun;
And bright, with borrow'd rays divine,
    Their glorious circuit run.

2 Beyond the reach of mortals spread
    Their light where'er they go;
And heav'nly influences shed
    O'er all the world below.

3 As the great Sun of righteousness,
    Their healing wings display,
And let their lustre still increase,
    Unto the perfect day.

4 And when their useful course is run
    Enjoy the kingdom giv'n;
Bright as the uncreated sun
    In the eternal heav'n.

CXIII. *For Exiles.*

⁎⁎ AN *outcast* from my native clime,
    Expell'd from friend and foe,
In this romantic *wild* confin'd
    My fate to undergo.

2 The former bleſſings I enjoy'd,
    While on my native ſhore,
With which I frequently was cloy'd,
    I now can taſte no more.

3 The table whereupon was laid
    The coſtly piles of meat,
Tho' then deſpis'd—I'd now be glad:
    Its meaneſt crumbs to eat.

4 My old companions in the time
    Of mirth and liberty,
Now that my wealth and pow'r decline,
    Have quite abandon'd me.

5 With poignant grief I call to mind
    My folly and exceſs;
For which I ſeek, but cannot find
    The ſmalleſt happineſs.

6 Deſerted here by ev'ry art,
    That leſſens human woe;
Compunction from my bleeding heart
    Continually does flow.

7 To whom in this dejected hour,
    For ſuccour can I flee?
But unto God, who by his pow'r,
    Alone can ſtrengthen me.

CXIV. *Morning.*

CXIV. *Morning.*

ON thee each *morning*, O my God!
    My waking thoughts attend,
On whom are founded all my hopes,
    And all my wishes end.

2 My soul, in pleasing wonder lost,
    His boundless love surveys;
And fir'd with grateful zeal, prepares
    Her sacrifice of praise.

3 He leads me thro' the maze of sleep,
    He brings me safe to light;
And with the same paternal care
    Conducts my steps till night.

4 When ev'ning slumbers press my eyes,
    With his protection blest;
In peace and safety I commit
    My weary limbs to rest.

5 My spirit in his hands secure,
    Fears no approaching ill;
For whether waking or asleep,
    The Lord is with me still.

6 I'll daily to th' astonish'd world,
    His wond'rous acts proclaim;
While all with me shall praises sing,
    With me shall bless his name.

CXV. *Affliction.*

*** O GOD! in mercy hear my pray'r,
    Regard a sinner's cry;
In this the hour of my *distress*,
    In pity, Lord, draw nigh.

2 From those that flatter'd still my hopes,
   I did expect relief;
But still their blasted schemes did tend
   To aggravate my *grief*.

3 I now with shame confess my guilt,
   Before thy presence, Lord,
That I could never once till now
   Believe thy faithful word.

4 Begone ye vain delusive dreams,
   Your counsel I repent;
'Tis only Jesus that can hear,
   And answer my complaint.

CXVI. *The Immensity of God.*

THOU dwell'st, O God, in radiant flame,
   Beyond our highest reach,
Thy nature and thy mighty name,
   Our minds and spirits teach.

2 The earth and seas divided were,
   By thine Almighty hand;
And winds and storms their wrath prepare,
   At thy divine command.

3 The pond'rous earth, the rolling spheres,
   Submit to thy decree;
A moment's time. a thousand years,
   Are both alike to thee.

4 Thy pow'r no agitation knows,
   Thy wisdom still the same,
Thy loving kindness always flows,
   In a perpetual stream.

5 Before

5 Before thee earth and hell submit
    As subject to thy call,
And devils, vanquish'd at thy feet,
    Confess thee all in all.

CXVII. *The Christian's Consolation.*

*** THRICE happy are the souls that mourn,
    And weep with godly fear;
Their Comforter shall soon return
    And dry up ev'ry tear.

2 The Father's dear and only Son,
    A sacrifice was made,
That he might for our guilt atone,
    By suff'ring in our stead.

3 Shielded by Christ's Almighty arm
    We Satan's rage endure,
And free from his destructive harm
    We rest ourselves secure.

4 Ere long we shall approach the end
    Of life's uncertain race,
Where we our endless years shall spend
    In everlasting peace.

5 There love and pleasure ever fill
    The soul with lasting joy;
There sin nor Satan never will
    Its happiness annoy.

CXVIII. *The Acceptable Sacrifice.*

WHEREWITH shall I approach the Lord,
    And bow before his throne?
Or how procure his kind regard,
    And for my guilt atone?

2 Shall thousand rams in flames expire,
    Will these his favours buy?
Or oil that should for holy fire,
    Ten thousand streams supply.

3 With trembling hands and bleeding heart,
    Should I my offspring slay:
Should this atone for ill-desert,
    And purge my guilt away?

4 Oh! no my soul, 'twere fruitless all,
    Such victims bleed in vain;
No fatlings from the field nor stall
    Such favours can obtain.

5 To men their *rights* I must allow,
    And proofs of *kindness* give;
To God with *humble rev'rence* bow,
    And to his glory live.

6 Hands that are clean, and hearts sincere,
    He never will despise:
And chearful duty he'll prefer
    To costly sacrifice.

CXIX. *Faith.*

*** IN hope of joys to us unknown,
    By *faith* we struggle here beneath;
'Till we obtain th' eternal crown,
    The end of persevering *faith.*

2 By faith we view the heav'nly prize,
    And bring celestial pleasures near:
Our *faith* the want of sight supplies,
    And does our drooping spirits chear.

3 Our *faith* superior to our sense,
    Displays as in our naked sight,
And is the brightest evidence
    Of things unseen by human light.

4 Thro' ev'ry desart here below,
    By *faith* and *hope* we urge our way;
Where winds and tempests hourly blow,
    'Till darkness brings an endless day.

5 But *faith* will soon be lost in sight,
    When here no more on earth confin'd;
When once the soul has wing'd its flight,
    And left this house of clay behind.

CXX. *Morning or Evening.*

HOSANNA, with a chearful sound,
    To God's upholding hand;
Ten thousand snares attend us round,
    And yet secure we stand.

2 That was a most amazing pow'r
    That rais'd us by a word,
And ev'ry day, and every hour,
    We lean upon the Lord.

3 The ev'ning rests our weary head,
    And angels guard the room;
We wake, and we admire the bed
    That was not made our tomb.

4 The rising morning can't ensure
    That we shall end the day;
For death stands ready at the door
    To take our lives away.

5 Our breath is forfeited by sin,
   To God's avenging law;
We own thy grace, immortal King,
   In ev'ry gasp we draw.

6 God is our sun, whose daily light
   Our joy and safety brings;
Our feeble flesh lies safe at night
   Beneath his shady wings.

CXXI. *The Intercession of Christ.*

*** JESUS our great Redeemer's gone
   To *plead* for us his dying blood;
He now appears before the throne,
   Our daily Advocate with God.

2 Whene'er our faint petitions rise
   Before our heav'nly Father's eye;
If Christ appears our sacrifice,
   Justice soon lays its veng'ance by.

3 Our pray'rs, our praise, and all our wants,
   To God, our Saviour still presents,
And he the blessing daily grants,
   Which our returning want prevents.

4 Ye trembling saints, lift up your voice;
   Ye sinners, now petitions bring;
Ye righteous in the Lord rejoice,
   Jesus your Advocate is King.

5 Not all the arts that Satan tries,
   Can ever faithful saints condemn,
For Jesus spreads his wounds and cries,
   I suffer'd *these* to *ransom* them.

CXXII. *Hell's*

CXXII. *Hell's Torments.*

IN the dark regions of the deep,
  Where devils rage, reserv'd in chains,
Despairing sinners howl and weep,
  Blaspheming God amidst their pains.

2 While wounded conscience will upbraid,
  And rend each guilty wretched breast,
Deserved veng'ance is display'd,
  Nor gives the soul a moment's rest:

3 Their gnawing worm shall never die,
  But gnaw them in eternal *flames*;
For wrath divine stands dreadful by,
  And rights of justice strictly claims.

4 The lake with brimstone ever burns,
  And endless clouds of smoke ascend;
While Diety incens'd returns
  Their deeds in torments without end.

5 Ye sinners, listen and beware;
  Flee from the fiery wrath to come;
Bow to the Saviour, and prepare
  To 'scape this endless fearful doom.

CXXIII. *The Divinity and Humanity of Christ.*

**BEFORE the starry frame was rear'd,
  Eternal was the *word*;
Before the sun and moon appear'd,
  As God *he* was ador'd.

2 Before revolving years began
    Their annual course to run:
Before that light began to dawn,
    Or yet the darkness shun.

3 Ere sin commenc'd, or Adam fell,
    Or devils waged war;
Jesus in glory did excel,
    The bright and morning star.

4 Yet such was his unbounded love
    For Adam's fallen race;
That, lo! he leaves his throne above
    To suffer in their place.

5 'Gainst man incensed justice storms,
    And aims the fatal blow;
But Christ, to save us dying worms,
    The *stroke* did undergo.

6 What Jesus suffer'd in our room,
    He suffer'd as a man;
Did *angel's* nature not assume,
    But that of *Abraham*.

CXXIV. *Satan's Temptations.*

BEWARE, my soul, of Satan's train;
    He takes his circuit round,
Content at first if he can gain,
    Tho' but an inch of ground.

2 He is thine enemy avow'd,
    His aim is to devour;
A duty left, a sin allow'd,
    Is his successful hour.

3 The place thy follies to him give,
    Will pain and sorrow cost;
Tho' grace from Christ thou dost receive,
    To balance what is lost.

4 Then, O my soul! thy ground maintain;
　　Courageously resist;
If stedfast thou thy faith retain,
　　The tempter will desist.

5 For Satan flees the Christian shield;
　　Nor can his sword endure;
They who stand fast, and never yield,
　　Their conquest is secure.

CXXV. *Scriptures.*

⁎ THE *sacred pages* of thy word,
　　O God, how bright they shine!
Thy precepts constantly afford
　　Unerring light divine.

2 Thy *word* diffuses light abroad,
　　In ev'ry humble mind;
Direction to thy blest abode,
　　In it we safely find.

3 When we thy *law* and *gospel* chuse,
　　Our only guides to be:
The more their precepts we peruse,
　　The more we know of thee.

4 Cause me to love thy holy *law*,
　　Make it my chief delight;
That from its *pages* I may draw,
　　A soul-reviving light.

5 'Tis in the annals of thy *book*,
　　That sure salvation lies;
'Tis thro' its *promises* we look
　　For life that never dies.

CXXVI. *Sorrows*

CXXVI. *Sorrows arising from Christ's Sufferings.*

ALAS! and did my Saviour bleed?
 And did my Sov'reign die?
Would he devote that sacred head,
 For such a worm as I?

2 Thy body slain, sweet Jesus, thine,
 And bath'd in its own blood;
While all expos'd to wrath divine,
 The glorious suff'rer stood.

3 Was it for crimes that I had done,
 He groan'd upon the tree?
Amazing pity! grace unknown!
 And love beyond degree!

4 Well might the sun in darkness hide,
 And shut his glories in,
When God the mighty Maker dy'd,
 For man the creature's sin.

5 Thus might I hide my blushing face,
 While his dear cross appears;
Dissolve my heart in thankfulness,
 And melt my eyes to tears.

CXXVII. *Sickness.*

*** AMIDST my death deserving sins,
 O Lord! remember me;
Afflictive *trouble* now begins
 To urge my flight to thee.

2 Let not thy wrath against me storm,
 For (O Almighty God!)
How can a weak and mortal worm
 Subsist beneath thy rod?

3 Increasing

3 Increasing *sickness*, pain and fear,
 Conspire to banish rest;
While from my eyes the flowing tear
 Are by my sorrows prest.

4 Thy pity, Lord, I now implore,
 Assuage my flowing grief;
And let it not be long before
 Thy mercy grant relief.

5 Hear, Jesus, for thy mercy's sake,
 My weak enfeebled cry;
When fainting dust and ashes speak,
 Thy healing balm apply.

6 Recruit my strength, and quickly ease
 The sorrows that I feel;
Thou only canst in this disease,
 My wasted body heal.

CXXVIII. *A Sinner's Prayer.*

BENEATH thy highly injur'd throne,
 Permit a wretch to lie:
O! may the gracious heav'ns drink up,
 My penitential cry.

2 Lord, break that dread entail of woe,
 Past in thy court above;
To pardon, is the highest act
 Done by the God of love.

3 To wreak just veng'ance on the head,
 Is but thy strange employ;
Nor unregretting can thine arm,
 Thy own hand-work destroy.

4 'Twould

4 'Twould counteract thy scheme of love,
    To mar my guilty frame,
Was't not to taste the cup of bless,
    That heaven rear'd the same.

5 Thy threats the flagrant rebel chace,
    'Till on his knees he yield;
But sure, thy royal word protects
    Him that gives up the field.

CXXIX. *Heaven.*

*** A HOUSE remains not made with hands,
    Reserv'd above the sky;
Where Jesus, my Redeemer, stands,
    My Advocate on high.

2 'Tis in this thrice delightful place,
    We rest from grief and sin;
And from the streams of endless grace,
    Drink lasting pleasures in.

3 'Till that important moment come,
    By faith we trust his word;
Believing that our present home,
    Is distant from the Lord.

4 By faith we view th' approaching hour,
    When pris'ners such as we;
On wings of love shall gladly tow'r,
    Our Father's house to see.

5 The heav'nly portals open'd wide,
    Shall then receive our soul;
To sit by our Redeemer's side,
    While endless ages roll.

CXXX. *Re-*

CXXX. *Resignation and Humility.*

ETERNAL Beam of light divine!
   Fountain of unexhausted love!
In whom the Father's glories shine,
   Thro' earth beneath and heav'n above.

2 Jesus, the weary wand'rer's rest,
   Give me thy easy yoke to bear;
With stedfast patience arm my breast,
   With spotless love and lowly fear.

3 Thankful I take the cup from thee,
   Prepar'd and mingled by thy skill,
Tho' bitter to the last it be,
   Pow'rful the wounded soul to heal.

4 Be thou, O Rock of ages! nigh,
   So shall each murm'ring thought be gone,
And grief, and fear, and care, shall fly
   As clouds before the mid-day sun.

5 Speak to my warring passions, "Peace;"
   Say to my trembling heart, "Be still:"
Thy pow'r my strength and fortress is,
   For all things serve thy sov'reign will.

6 O death! where is thy sting? Where now
   Thy boasted victory. O grave?
Who shall contend with God? or who
   Can hurt, whom God delights to save?

CXXXI. *Morning.*

*** MINE eyes behold the rising sun:
   What life his rays convey!
Rejoicing still his course to run,
   'Till darkness ends the day.

2 With pleasure from my bed I rise,
  Forget the shades of night :
Exulting, place my ravish'd eyes
  Upon the beams of light.

3 O thou! to whose protecting pow'r
  I owe my vital breath,
Upheld by thee, I live this hour,
  Amidst the shafts of death.

4 O may the pow'r that did protect
  My slumbers where I lay !
In loving-kindness still direct
  My steps throughout the day.

5 Conduct thro' life's uncertain race
  My soul from danger free,
'Till I, thro' thy Almighty grace,
  Shall wing my flight to thee.

CXXXII. *Humility.*

TO thee, O God! I hourly sigh,
  But not for golden stores ;
Nor covet I the brighest gems,
  On the rich eastern shores.

2 Nor that deluding empty joy,
  Men call a mighty name,
Nor greatness in its gayest pride,
  My restless thoughts enflame.

3 Nor pleasures soft enticing charms
  My fond desires allure :
Far greater things than these from thee
  My wishes would secure.

4 Those

4 Those blisful, those transporting smiles,
    That brighten heav'n above,
The boundless riches of thy grace,
    And treasures of thy love.

5 These are the mighty things I want,
    O! make these blessings mine;
And I the glories of the world
    Contentedly resign.

CXXXIII. *Mariners.*

*** O! YE who foreign climes explore,
    Assisted by the waves and wind,
Where stormy seas and tempests roar,
    Your Sov'reign Pilot hourly mind.

2 That God, to whom you make your cry,
    Demands your greatest thanks and praise,
Who has, when seeming death was nigh,
    Still lengthen'd out your helpless days.

3 To him that bade the seas assuage,
    And wall'd her round on ev'ry side;
Who made the waves forget their rage,
    And rain'd secure the foaming tide.

4 To him your grateful homage pay,
    Who sav'd your near expiring breath,
Whose voice the winds and seas obey,
    Who freed you from impending death.

5 O! ye that plow the raging main,
    The Lord of earth and seas adore:
His name nor sabbaths ne'er profane,
    Whose pow'r conducts you safe to shore.

CXXXIV. *Public*

CXXXIV. *Public Worship.*

COME, let us use the grace divine,
    And all with one accord,
In a perpetual cov'nant join
    Ourselves to Christ the Lord.

2 Give up ourselves thro' Jesus' pow'r,
    His name to glorify,
And promise in this sacred hour
    For God to live and die.

3 The cov'nant we this moment make,
    Be ever kept in mind:
We will no more our God forsake,
    Nor cast his words behind.

4 We never will throw off his fear,
    Who hears our solemn vow;
And if thou art well pleas'd to hear,
    Come down and meet us now.

CXXXV. *Love and Charity.*

. GENTLE and peaceful, as a dove,
    Let me from strife and envy cease,
Let me still imitate the love
    And meekness of the Prince of Peace.

2 Thro' the whole tenor of my life
    Let love and mercy daily run,
But enmity and jarring strife,
    Teach me with anxious care to shun.

3 Whatever system I esteem,
    Or sect or party do approve,
My whole religion is a dream,
    If void of *charity* or *love*.

4 Altho'

4 Altho' in sentiment disjoin'd,
    And lesser points we differ broad,
I'll love the man, whoe'er I find,
    That loves, believes, and fears his God:

5 With this inscription on my heart,
    I'll *love* and *charity* pursue,
'Till ev'ry sect, in ev'ry part,
    Be all reduc'd to only TWO.§

CXXXVI. *Judgment.*

THOU Judge of quick and dead,
    Before whose bar severe,
With holy joy or guilty dread,
    We all shall soon appear:
    Our caution'd souls prepare,
    For that tremendous *day*,
And fill us now with watchful care,
    And stir us up to pray.

2 To pray and wait the *hour*,
    That awful *hour* unknown,
When rob'd in majesty and pow'r,
    Thou shalt from heav'n come down,
    Th' immortal Son of man,
    To *judge* the human race,
With all thy Father's dazzling train,
    With all thy glorious grace.

3 To damp our earthly joys,
    T' increase our gracious fears,
For ever let th' Archangel's voice
    Be sounding in our ears:

§ Viz. Children of God, and children of the Devil.

The solemn mid-night cry,
"Ye dead, the Judge is come,
"Arise and meet him in the sky,
"And meet your instant doom!"
4 O may we thus be found
  Obedient to his word,
Attentive to the trumpet's sound,
  And looking for our Lord!
  O may we thus ensure
  A lot among the blest,
And watch a moment to secure
  An everlasting rest!

CXXXVII. *Affliction.*

*** MY God, to thee for help I fly,
    Thy pow'r in my behalf exert;
This hour my fainting soul stand by,
    Reviving strength to me impart.
2 Surround, uphold, and strengthen me,
    Defend me by thy mighty arm,
And while my pray'r ascends to thee,
    Protect me from impending harm.
3 Alarming dangers now appear,
    Around my soul they hourly fly,
O! fill my mind with godly fear,
    O! save me, Jesus, or I die.
4 To me, thy guardian mercy shew,
    Thy fortifying pow'r and grace;
That I, secure from all below,
    Beneath thy wings may rest in peace.

5 Jesus,

5 Jesus, the weary sinner's friend,
  My soul ascends to thee in pray'r;
On thee for all things I depend,
  Secure me from the tempter's snare.

CXXXVIII. *The Goodness of God.*

THY heav'nly blessings, dearest Lord,
  My grateful lips employ;
And constantly my thoughts afford
  A heart reviving joy.

2 Thro' all my life's uncertain stage
  Thy providence I see,
While from my foe's Satanic rage,
  Thy goodness sets me free.

3 When want and indigence combine,
  To heighten my distress;
That never failing *grace* of thine,
  Does then to me increase.

4 If sickness does my health assail,
  And death approaches nigh;
Thy *love* and *mercy* never fail
  To hear me when I cry.

5 If thro' the business of the day
  My weary frame's opprest,
Thy nightly *comforts* still supply
  My soul with balmy rest.

6 Thus ev'ry where I daily prove
  Thy watchful care of me,
Secure within thy arms of love,
  From ev'ry danger free.

CXXXIX. *The Death of Christ, &c.*

HE *dies!* the friend of sinners *dies!*
   Lo! Salem's daughters weep around!
A solemn darkness veils the skies!
   A sudden trembling shakes the ground.
Come saints, and drop a tear of woe,
   For him who groan'd beneath your load,
He shed a thousand drops for you,
   A thousand drops of richer blood.

2 Here's love and grief beyond degree,
   The Lord of glory dies for men;
But, lo! with sudden joy we see!
   Jesus the dead revives again!
The rising God forsakes the tomb,
   (The tomb in vain forbids his rise)
Cherubic legions guard him home,
   And shout him welcome to the skies.

3 Break off your tears, ye saints, and tell,
   How high our great Deliv'rer reigns;
Sing how he spoil'd the hosts of hell,
   And led the monster death in chains.
Say, "Live for ever, wond'rous King,
   "Born to redeem, and strong to save!"
Then ask the tyrant, "Where's thy sting?"
   And where's thy vict'ry, boasting grave?

CXL. *Servants.*

⁎⁎⁎ THOU who a servant didst become,
   To do thy Father's will,
Teach me that I, like thee, my task,
   May constantly fulfil.

2 Dear God, who, when thou waſt deſpis'd,
    Didſt never once repine;
O teach me ſtill to imitate
    That humble heart of thine.

3 If I am faithful unto death,
    My conqueſt is ſecure;
I ſhall attain a crown of life,
    For ever to endure.

4 In that eternal houſe above,
    Gold cannot bribe a ſeat,
The poor (if pious) there are on
    A level with the great.

5 If he the talent well improves,
    Which he receives from thee,
The meaneſt *ſervant* here on earth,
    Shall as his maſter be!

CXLI. *Evening.*

THE morn is paſt, the noon-tide o'er,
    And the declining ſun,
Obedient to creative pow'r,
    His ſteady courſe has run.

2 Perhaps no more on earth to riſe,
    At leaſt to riſe on me,
The cloſe of night may cloſe my eyes
    To all eternity.

3 Reflect, my ſoul, the days and years,
    The hours of dark account,
Trifling purſuits, and fruitleſs cares,
    To what do they amount!

4 If I have err'd, instruct to mourn,
    To give each fault a tear;
Hopeless of peace, till my return
    Hath found forgiveness there.

5 Thy mercies still thou dost impart,
    With ev'ry added day,
Above the rest, O! give an heart
    Its tribute still to pay.

6 O thou! whose favour more I prize
    Than all beneath the sky,
Say I am thine, it shall suffice,
    And I can smile and die.

CXLII. *The Faithfulness of God.*

THO' troubles assail, and dangers affright,
    Tho' friends should all fail, and foes all unite,
Yet one thing secures us, whatever betide,
The *promise* assures us, *the Lord will provide.*

2 Thy call we obey, like Abram of old,
We know not the way, but faith makes us bold,
Altho' we are strangers, we have a sure guide,
And trust in all dangers, *the Lord will provide.*

3 We all may, like ships, with tempests be tost,
On perilous deeps, but need not be lost;
Tho' Satan enrages the wind and the tide,
Yet scripture engages, *the Lord will provide.*

4 When Satan appears to stop up our path,
Or fill us with fears, we triumph by faith;
He cannot take from us, altho' he's oft tried,
That heart chearing promise, *the Lord will provide.*

5. When

5 When life sinks apace, and death is in view,
The word of thy grace shall carry us through,
Nor fearing nor doubting with Christ on our side,
We hope to die shouting, *the Lord will provide.*

CXLIII. *The Incarnation of Christ.*

*** AMAZING grace to man appears,
    Let saints rejoice and sing;
Behold! for us a virgin bears
    A Saviour and a King.

2 Attending angels from on high,
    Proclaim, with holy mirth,
To watching shepherds, where they ly,
    The tidings of his birth.

3 Directed by an orient star,
    The sages find their road,
'Till safely they conducted were
    To the incarnate God.

4 What love and wonder now begin
    To fill our ravish'd eyes;
While we behold our King within
    The manger where he lies.

5 Jesus, thou wondrous God and man,
    How does thy glory shine?
What love or meekness ever can
    Be equal, Lord, to thine?

CXLIV. *A Sinner's Wish.*

AGAIN, indulgent Lord, I come;
  Again to tell my wants presume;
I want to know thee as thou art,
I want to find thee in my heart.

                2 I want

2 I want to feel I die to sin;
I would no longer live therein:
No earthly bliss can do me good;
I want the balm of Jesus' blood.

3 I want acquaintance with the Lamb,
To know the virtues of his name;
I want assurance of my faith;
I want a conquest over death.

4 I want to be made free indeed,
To trample on the serpent's head,
I want my wants to be supply'd,
And have ten thousand wants beside,

5 I want myself and wants to know;
I want in faith and hope to grow;
I want *thyself!* this favour grant,
And thou hast granted all I want.

CXLV. *The Patience of God.*

*** HOW *patient* is Almighty God!
    And unto anger flow;
How long does he *suspend* the rod,
    O'er sinners here below!

2 How patiently Jehovah stands,
    And unto sinners cries,
" Accept of pardon from my hands,
    " Life in the favour lies?"

3 God in a mild and gentle way,
    His mercy does intrude;
And man the favour does repay,
    With his ingratitude.

4 The ox obeys the galling yoke,
    And knows his master's stall;
While men Almighty God provoke,
    Despising ev'ry call.

5 But this decree in heav'n's past,
    For God himself has sworn,
Insulted patience will at last
    To endless fury turn.

CXLVI. *The Hiding-Place*, Isaiah xxxii. 2.

HAIL, boundless love that first began
    The scheme to rescue fallen man!
Hail, matchless, free, eternal grace,
That gave my soul a *hiding-place!*

2 Against the God who rules the sky
I fought, with hands uplifted high;
Despis'd the motions of his grace,
Too proud to seek a *hiding-place.*

3 Enwrap'd in thick Egyptian night,
And fond of darkness more than light,
Madly I ran the sinful race,
Secure without a *hiding-place.*

4 But when thy Spirit's mighty pow'r,
At last unbolted mercy's door,
I plainly saw my wretched case,
And found I had no *hiding-place.*

5 E'er long, an heav'nly voice I heard,
And mercy's angel-form appear'd;
She led me on with placid pace,
To *Jesus* as my *hiding-place.*

6 Should

6 Should storms of dreadful thunder roll,
And shake the globe from pole to pole;
No flaming bolt could daunt my face,
For *Jesus* is my *hiding-place*.

7 A few more rolling suns, at most,
Will land me safe on Canaan's coast,
Where I shall sing the song of grace,
And see my glorious *hiding-place*.

CXLVII. *Scriptures.*

WHEN quiet in my house I sit,
    Thy *book* be my companion still:
My joy, thy sayings to repeat,
    Talk o'er the records of thy will.

2 O! may the gracious *words* divine,
    Subject of all my converse be:
So will the Lord his follow'rs join,
    And walk, and talk himself with me.

3 Oft as I lay me down to rest,
    O may the reconciling *word*
Sweetly compose my weary breast,
    While on the bosom of my Lord.

4 Rising to sing my Saviour's praise
    Thee may I publish all day long,
And let thy precious *words* of grace
    Flow from my heart and fill my tongue.

CXLVIII. *Old Age.*

***O THOU! who, from my infant years,
    Hast guarded ev'ry hour;
Uphold me now, that death appears,
    By thy Almighty pow'r.

2 Thess:

These feeble limbs of mine declare
  My journey here is run;
These wither'd hands bid me prepare
  For my eternal home.

3 These hoary locks, as silver gray,
  To me they hourly call,
" See how we vanish and decay
  " As leaves in autumn fall."

4 In vain each object courts my sight,
  Before these languid eyes;
Tho' aided by the clearest light,
  That shines thro' azure skies.

5 All bliss is fled of ev'ry kind;
  My Maker wills it so:
I cannot long remain behind
  A tenant here below.

6 When death commands this mortal clay
  To mingle with the dust,
Lord, aid my soul to wing its way
  To mansions of the just.

CXLIX. *Happiness.*

THRICE blessed are the humble hearts
  That mourn the follies they have done,
To them a gracious God imparts
  Salvation thro' his only Son.

Internal joy their minds possess,
  While Jesus dwells their hearts within;
And as their faith and love increase,
  They find their heav'n on earth begin.

3 Their Father hears their fervent cries,
    Guides and conducts their future lives;
As Satan's kingdom in them dies,
    So Jesus' kingdom still revives.

4 With calm and undisturbed peace,
    Their lasting pleasures never cloy,
Progressively they feel his grace
    Reviving ev'ry spring of joy.

5 If they are faithful unto death,
    And still their talents here improve;
E'er they resign their vital breath,
    They *antedate* the joys above.

CL. *A Prayer.*

I WANT a principle within
    Of jealous godly fear,
A sensibility of sin,
    A pain to feel it near.

2 That I no more from thee may part,
    No more thy goodness grieve,
The filial awe, the fleshly heart,
    The tender conscience give.

3 Quick as the apple of an eye,
    O God! my conscience make;
Awake my soul when sin is nigh,
    And keep it still awake.

4 If to the right or left I stray,
    That moment, Lord, reprove;
And let me weep my life away,
    For having griev'd thy love.

5 O! may the least omission pain
    My well-instructed soul;
And drive me to the blood again,
    Which makes the wounded whole.

CLI. *Ubiquity.*

*** FROM him who fills unbounded space,
    Where can a sinner run?
Or where's the dark and hiding-place
    That can his notice shun?

2 If rising with the morning sky
    I wing my early flight,
If with the sun I quickly fly,
    Shall these evade his sight?

3 If still attempting my escape
    To heav'n I do aspire;
Or to the shades of darkness leap,
    And dwell in liquid fire.

4 Yet *there* his presence is display'd,
    In beams of love divine;
And *here* in dreadful pomp array'd,
    His wrath and justice shine.

5 For still on ev'ry hand the pow'r
    Of God I plainly trace,
Where'er I vainly think to tow'r,
    Throughout infinite space.

CLII. *The Power of God.*

'TWAS God that tun'd the rolling spheres,
    And stretch'd the winding skies;
That form'd the plan of endless years,
    And bade the angels rise.

2 From everlasting is his might,
    Unbounded, unconfin'd,
He pierces thro' the realms of light,
    And rides upon the wind.

3 The sun shrinks back as he appears,
    The moon forgets to shine;
And ev'ry blasted star declares
    His majesty divine.

4 He speaks; great nature's wheels stand still,
    And cease their wonted round;
The mountains melt, each trembling hill
    Forgets its ancient bound.

5 He scatters nations with his breath,
    The scatter'd nations fly;
Blue pestilence and spreading death
    Confess the God-head high.

CLIII. *Evening.*

*** To him, whose mercy thro' the day,
    Conducts us safe to night,
This ev'ning sacrifice we pay,
    For his protecting might.

2 Dangers against us still conspire,
    In artful guise array'd;
But round us as a wall of fire,
    His mercies are display'd.

3 To thy supreme protecting pow'r,
    Our grateful thanks we owe;
Whose boundless mercy ev'ry hour
    Conducts our steps below.

4 Now

4 Now Father, to thy guardian love
    Our spirits we commend;
Receive us to thy throne above,
    When life shall have an end.

CLIV. *Death.*

LIFE, like an empty vapour flies,
    A fable, or a song,
By swift degrees our nature dies,
    Nor can our joys be long.

2 'Tis but a few whose days amount
    To threescore years and ten,
And all beyond that short account
    Are sorrow, toil, and pain.

3 Our vitals with laborious strife
    Bear up the crazy load,
And drag those poor remains of life
    Along the tiresome road.

4 Almighty God reveal thy love,
    And not thy wrath alone;
O! let our sweet experience prove
    The mercies of thy throne.

5 Our souls would learn the heav'nly art,
    T''improve the hours we have,
That we may act the wiser part,
    And live beyond the grave.

CLV. *Public Worship.*

*** THOU sacred spring of life, before thine eyes
We would present our guilt and sore distress,
Our daily crimes ascend above the skies,
    Against thy love, and still forbearing grace.

To thee, O Saviour! to thy blood alone
  We fly, to make our broken spirits whole;
Thy all-sufficient merit can atone,
  For all the sins of each diseased soul.

Before thy presence here we guilty stand,
  Let not thy gracious Spirit quite depart,
In mercy, Lord, apply thy healing hand;
  O! write forgiveness on each waiting heart.

CLVI. *A Prayer——by a Friend.*

O! THOU high thron'd above all height,
  To whom angelic hosts shall raise,
With boundless ever new delight,
  Celestial songs of love and praise.

2 Cloathed with majesty and might,
  In wisdom, as in pow'r supreme,
First cause of all, great source of light,
  Of life, of joys, devoid of pain.

3 Teach me with all thy creatures now,
  In adoration low to fall,
Humbly to feel, and joy, that thou
  Alone, O Lord, art all in all.

CLVII. *The Crucifixion of Christ.*

*** JESUS, the friend of sinners, see,
  Attend his groaning sighs!
Cover'd with blood, on yonder tree,
  The sacred victim dies.

2 His dying groans all nature shake,
  While light'nings flash around,
The frighted rocks in sunder break,
  Alarmed at the sound.

3 The rolling sun his God bemoans,
    Asham'd he hides his face,
While bursting thunder loudly groans,
    Lamenting his disgrace.

4 Sure angels wept in tears of blood,
    The light its beams deny'd,
While only man supinely stood,
    For whose offence he dy'd!

CLVIII. *A National Fast.*

SEE, gracious God, before thy throne
    Thy mourning people bend!
'Tis on thy sov'reign grace alone
    Our humble hopes depend.

2 Tremend'ous judgments from thy hand,
    Thy dreadful pow'r display:
Yet mercy spares this guilty land,
    And still we live to pray.

3 What num'rous crimes increasing rise
    Thro' this apostate isle!
What land so favour'd of the skies,
    And yet what land so vile!

4 Regardless of thy smile or frown,
    Their pleasures they require;
And sink with gay indiff'rence, down
    To everlasting fire.

5 O! turn thou us, Almighty Lord,
    By thy unbounded grace;
Then shall our hearts receive thy word,
    And humbly seek thy face.

6 Then, should insulting foes invade,
   We need not yield to fear;
Assur'd of never-failing aid,
   If thou, our God, art near.

CLIX. *Creation.*

⁎⁎* ADORE th' amazing pow'r of God,
   Who bade the hills arise,
Extend the praise of him abroad,
   That spread the starry skies.

2 He fram'd at first the flying clouds,
   By his Almighty hand;
The ample fields, and liquid floods,
   Obey his great command.

3 Ordain'd by his creative pow'r,
   The sun must rule the day,
While all the planets in their tour,
   His sov'reign will obey.

4 He form'd the plants and flow'rs below,
   Which all the fields array'd:
In all the winds and storms that blow,
   His wonders are display'd.

5 The creatures both in sea and land,
   Are objects of his care,
And from his all-supporting hand,
   Perpetual blessings share.

CLX. *Public Worship.*

O COME let us join, in music divine,
   The Saviour to laud,
      'Tis meet and fit,
It is charming, and perfectly sweet,
The Saviour to praise, our Lord and our God,
                                    'Tis

'Tis a pleasure to sing, of a crucify'd King
   With courage and flame.
The angels that love us, and seraphs above us,
   Do always the same.
Hark! hark! how they shout, all heaven throughout
   In sounding his name.

CLXI. *Repentance and Humility.*

**IN boundless mercy Lord, forgive
   A sinner such as me,
O! let a vanquish'd rebel live
   In favour, Lord, with thee.

2 Condemn'd, I stand before thy face,
   Involv'd in guilt and sin;
Thou justly might'st with-hold thy grace,
   And leave me still therein.

3 But yet in wrath, remember, Lord,
   My penitential cry,
And ev'ry promise of thy word
   Unto my soul apply.

4 Let not my sighings prove in vain,
   Nor yet my flowing tears;
But wash my soul from ev'ry stain,
   And ease my doubting fears.

CLXII. *Scriptures.*

GREAT God, with wonder and with praise,
   On all thy works I look,
But still thy wisdom, pow'r, and grace,
   Shine brighter in thy book.

2 The stars that in their courses roll,
    Have much instruction giv'n;
But still thy word informs my soul,
    How I may climb to heav'n.

3 The fields provide me food, and show
    The goodness of the Lord;
But fruits of life and glory grow
    In thy most blessed word.

4 Here are my choicest treasures hid;
    And here my comfort lies;
Here my desires are satisfied,
    And hence my hopes arise.

5 Make me to love thy precepts more,
    And take a fresh delight
By day to read these wonders o'er,
    And meditate by night.

CLXIII. *Heaven.*

*** ARISE my soul, and quickly fly,
    Thy race of duty run;
See how they live with God on high,
    Beyond the rising sun.

2 No ev'ning shades, no gloomy nights,
    Disturb their peaceful rest;
Still tasting ever fresh delights,
    They live entirely blest.

3. Within these sacred courts above,
    No sorrows enter in;
Surrounded by Almighty love,
    Secure from death and sin.

4 Each

4 Each tenant there forgets his toil,
    His former doubts and fears;
Whilst beams of endless mercy smile,
    To wipe away their tears.

5 Dear Saviour, guide me to that day
    Which shall my soul remove
Far distant from this house of clay,
    To worship thee above.

CLXIV. *The Love and Patience of Christ.*

**BEHOLD your dear Redeemer stands,
    For you he spreads his bleeding hands,
      His rebels to receive:
For you his wounds are open'd wide,
The language of his streaming side
      Still bids you turn and live.

2 He now is knocking at your heart,
The purchas'd blessing to impart
      To ev'ry humble mind:
Whoever hears, and thus complies,
And turns his heart from Satan's ways,
      Shall grace and glory find.

3 This heav'nly guest in patience waits;
Long has he stood without your gates,
      Repuls'd by Satan's pow'r:
While Jesus does this visit pay,
No more his proffer'd love deny,
      But know your gracious hour.

4 If now before his throne ye fall,
Submissive to your Maker's call,

And to the end endure:
If ye increase in faith and love,
Your title to the crown above,
And conquest are secure.

CLXV. *Old Age.*

MY God, my everlasting hope,
 I live upon thy truth:
Thy hands have held my childhood up,
 And strengthen'd all my youth.

2 My flesh was fashion'd by thy pow'r,
 With all these limbs of mine:
And from my mother's painful hour,
 I've been entirely thine.

3 Still has my life new wonders seen,
 Repeated ev'ry year:
Behold my days that yet remain,
 I trust them to thy care.

4 Cast me not off when strength declines,
 When hoary hairs arise;
And round me let thy glory shine,
 Whene'er thy servant dies.

5 Then in the hist'ry of my age,
 When men review my days,
They'll read thy love in ev'ry page,
 In ev'ry line thy praise.

CLXVI. *The Goodness of God.*

⁂ MY God, my Saviour, and my King,
 Assist me to prepare
The praise which to thy throne I bring,
 To find acceptance there.

2 To thee belongs my grateful song,
    For all thy love to me;
Yea, greater praises than my tongue
    Can offer, Lord, to thee.

3 What favours bless'd my infant soul,
    Before I understood
They came from thee, the endless source
    Of never failing good?

4 Thou didst thro' each revolving year,
    For all my wants provide,
In my distress I found thee near,
    My guardian and my guide.

5 But when I raise my thoughts on high,
    To endless life above,
How should my spirit magnify
    Thy undeserved love.

6 Now since thy mercies ever give,
    Such blessings unto me,
O! may I rather cease to live,
    Than cease from loving thee.

CLXVII. *Longing to be with Jesus.*

I LONG my Redeemer to see,
    My Jesus above to behold;
The Saviour who suffer'd for me,
    Surrounded by harpers on gold;
My Master in glory to meet,
    To gaze on his heavenly face;
With rapture to fall at his feet,
    And share in the triumphs of grace.

2 Ah! why does thy chariot delay
    To waft me where sin is no more?
Come, Lord, and in mercy convey
    My soul to that heavenly shore,
Where holy, and perfect, and pure,
    My glorify'd spirit shall sing;
My body for ever endure,
    And shout to my crucify'd King.

3 To think on this day of thy love,
    Which all my distresses shall crown,
My sorrows for ever remove,
    And death in its victory drown;
It makes me resign'd to my grief,
    While, yet a few moments, I know
O'er Jordan, my spirit's relief,
    To Jesus's bosom I go.

CLXVIII. *Mariners at Sea.*

⁎⁎FATHER, thy mercy we implore,
    Our lives in safety keep;
Conduct us to our native shore,
    Along this floating deep.

2 Great Ruler of the raging sea,
    Whose voice the waves obey;
With thankful hearts we here to thee
    Our grateful homage pay.

3 Thy pow'r and majesty appear
    Throughout the foaming brine,
And still we find, when danger's near,
    That guardian love of thine.

4 Tho'

4 Tho' winds enrage the flowing tide,
 Tho' seas in mountains rise;
Yet in thy goodness we'll confide,
 Thou Lord of sea and skies.

CLXIX. *The Goodness of God.*

FATHER, how wide thy glory shines,
 How high thy wonders rise,
Known thro' the earth by thousand signs,
 By thousands thro' the skies.

2 Those mighty orbs proclaim thy pow'r,
 Their motions speak thy skill:
And on the wings of ev'ry hour
 We read thy patience still.

3 But when we view thy strange design
 To save rebellious worms,
Where veng'ance and compassion join
 In their divinest forms:

4 Here the whole Deity is known,
 Nor dares a creature guess
Which of the glories brightest shone,
 The justice or the grace.

CLXX. *Youth.*

⁂ ATTEND to this important truth,
 Ye gay, of tender years;
On whom the rosy dawn of youth,
 In all its bloom appears.

2 'Tis now the snares of life array
 Themselves in borrow'd hue,
And flatt'ring pleasures ev'ry day
 In joyful mood ye view.

3 Deaf

3 Deaf to the monitor within,
  Your passions ye obey;
And slaves to ev'ry ruling sin,
  Ye own their baneful sway.

4 But mind that pleasure soon will pall,
  The blooming flow'r may blast,
And leaves or autumn too may fall,
  And die and wither fast.

5 In virtue now your minds improve;
  For 'tis a certain truth,
That early virtues always prove
  An ornament to youth.

6 To him who rear'd your infant frame,
  By his paternal care,
A grateful tribute for the same,
  With thankful hearts prepare.

CLXXI. *The Language of Faith.*

A CHARGE to keep I have;
  A God to glorify;
A never-dying soul to save,
  And fit it for the sky.

2 To serve the present age,
  My calling to fulfil;
O! may it all my pow'rs engage
  To do my Master's will.

3 Arm me with jealous care,
  As in thy sight to live,
And O! thy servant, Lord, prepare
  A strict account to give.

4 Help

4 Help me to watch and pray,
 And on thyself rely;
Assur'd, if I my trust betray,
 I shall for ever die.

CLXXII. *Judgment.*

⁎ AN angel from the rending sky
 On flaming wings appears;
His trumpet's loud majestic cry
 Is founding in our ears.

2 Nor those alone on earth that dwell,
 Are fill'd with awful dread;
For lo! 'tis heard thro' ev'ry cell,
 And mansion of the dead.

3 The tenants of the grave arise,
 And break the bars of night,
And view with their new open'd eyes,
 The long extinguish'd light.

4 Before the Judge' tribunal seat
 The assembled world stand,
To take their last decisive fate
 From his impartial hand.

5 Who did their faith by virtue prove,
 Ascend with him to heav'n;
While those who scorn'd redeeming love,
 Are from his presence driv'n.

CLXXIII. *Trust in God.*

WHILE thee I seek, protecting pow'r!
 Be my vain wishes still'd;
And may this consecrated hour
 With better hopes be fill'd.

2 Thy love the pow'rs of thought bestow'd,
   To thee my thoughts would soar;
Thy mercy o'er my life has flow'd,
   That mercy I adore.

3 In each event of life, how clear
   Thy ruling hand I see;
Each blessing to my soul more dear,
   Because conferr'd by thee.

4 In ev'ry joy that crowns my days,
   In ev'ry pain I bear,
My heart shall find delight in praise,
   Or seek relief in pray'r.

5 When gladness wings my favour'd hour,
   Thy love my thoughts shall fill,
Resign'd, when storms of sorrows lour,
   My soul shall meet thy will.

6 My lifted eye without a tear,
   The louring storm shall see;
My stedfast heart shall know no fear,
   That heart will rest on thee.

CLXXIV. *Universal Praise to God.*

⁂ LET heav'n, and earth, and seas combine,
   And tune the sacred lyre,
To praise eternal pow'r divine,
   In one united choir.

2 Ye angels, foremost sons of light,
   Ye saints, a shining throng,
Ye sun, ye regents of the night,
   Conspire to raise the song.

3 Ye higheſt heav'ns, his dread abode,
  Ye clouds and winds agree
To praiſe, with holy mirth, the God
  That formed earth and ſea.

4 Ye vallies low, ye flow'ry plains,
  Ye tow'ring mountains high,
Unite to praiſe, in chearful ſtrains,
  The Sov'reign of the ſky.

5 Ye dragons, and ye deeps below,
  Ye tenants of the ſtream,
Ye liquid fire, ye feather'd ſnow,
  Revere his mighty name.

6 Let old and young, in ev'ry ſtage,
  The ſacred theme employ,
From blooming youth to fading age,
  With univerſal joy.

7 Let ev'ry ſoul enraptur'd join,
  Before his throne appear,
T' adore his Majeſty divine,
  With reverential fear.

8 To his benign paternal care,
  His num'rous creatures owe,
Whatever gifts we mortals ſhare
  Of happineſs below.

9 Whoe'er his favour ſtill implores,
  His mercies ever crown,
And from his never-fading ſtores,
  Pour endleſs bleſſings down.

10 The meaneſt inſect that his pow'r
    Has made to creep or fly,
His gracious goodneſs ev'ry hour
    Does all its wants ſupply.

11 While higheſt ſeraphs round his throne,
    Who on his will attend,
Declare, that they on him alone
    Do conſtantly depend.

CLXXV. *Morning.*

ONCE more, my ſoul, the riſing day
    Salutes thy waking eyes;
Once more, my voice, thy tribute pay
    To him that rules the ſkies.

2 Night unto night his name repeats,
    The day renews the ſound,
Wide as the heav'ns on which he ſits,
    To turn the ſeaſons round.

3 'Tis he ſupports my mortal frame;
    My tongue ſhall ſpeak his praiſe:
My ſins would rouſe his wrath to flame,
    And ſtill his wrath delays.

4 On a poor worm thy pow'r might tread,
    And I could ne'er withſtand;
Thy juſtice might have cruſh'd me dead,
    But mercy held thine hand.

5 A thouſand wretched ſouls are fled
    Since the laſt ſetting ſun,
And yet thou length'neſt out my thread,
    And lets my moments run.

6 Dear God, let all my hours be thine,
   Whilst I enjoy the light;
Then shall my sun in smiles decline,
   And bring a pleasing night.

CLXXVI. *Masters.*

⁂ TO thee my God, my gracious King,
   I now present this sacrifice;
Myself and household here I bring,
   To find acceptance in thine eyes.

2 Within my tent, O God, reside,
   And teach me by thy heav'nly grace;
Let thy unerring wisdom guide
   My life in holiness and peace.

3 Let me the bright example give,
   That all my household plain may see,
How they, to thee, might daily live,
   And regulate their lives by me.

4 The pious servant and the just,
   Within my house I'll still retain;
And shall with confidential trust,
   Him always cherish and esteem.

5 The graceless, scoffing, and profane,
   Or them that frequent lies do tell,
With those that take thy name in vain,
   Beneath my roof shall never dwell.

6 Thus, sin and sinners ev'ry where,
   Shall still be banish'd far from me,
'Till I my house and heart prepare,
   As dwellings fit for lodging thee.

CLXXVII. *Preservation thro' Christ.*

GOD of my life, whose gracious pow'r,
    Thro' various deaths my soul hath led,
Or turn'd aside the fatal hour;
    Or lifted up my sinking head!

2 In all my ways thy hand I own,
    Thy ruling providence I see;
Assist me still my course to run,
    And still direct my paths to thee.

3 Oft hath the *sea* confest thy pow'r,
    And giv'n me back at thy command:
It could not, Lord, my life devour,
    Safe in the hollow of thine hand.

4 Oft from the margin of the *grave*,
    Thou, Lord, hast lifted up my head;
Sudden I found thee near to save;
    The fever own'd thy touch, and fled.

5 Whither, O whither, should I fly,
    But to my loving Saviour's breast?
Secure within thine arms to lie,
    And safe beneath thy wings to rest!

CLXXVIII. *Old Age.*

*** ALMIGHTY Ruler of the sky,
    Whom heav'n and earth adore;
Who still regard'st the humble cry,
    Thy mercy I implore.

2 Conduct me thro' my *aged years*,
    To my expiring hour;
And when my latest foe appears,
    Support me by thy pow'r.

3 I soon must render up my trust;
    My wasting strength impairs:
To mingle with its ancient dust,
    My body now prepares.

4 My pleasures now how quick they fly,
    Like to my ebbing sand,
And loudly cry, "The time of my
    Departure is at hand."

5 When death asunder breaks the bands,
    Which soul and body join,
Great God! into thy gracious hands
    Receive this soul of mine.

6 O thou! on whose Almighty pow'r
    My confidence depends;
Support me in that awful hour,
    When *dust* to *dust* descends!

END OF PART FIRST.

PART SECOND.

POEMS,

MORAL AND DIVINE.

PIETY AND POLITENESS,

A Dialogue*.

⁎⁎ THE sun had finish'd his diurnal toil,
And Cynthia fill'd her silver lamp with oil:
Array'd in all the pomp of borrow'd light,
Her beams dispell'd the horrors of the night:
The tinged sky was starr'd with beamy gold,
And swains immur'd their herds in ev'ry fold.

---

* The Author's intention in this Dialogue is to unite the Gentleman and the Christian, or godliness and good-manners together; as he frequently observes, with regret, many who profess the one are but too indifferently attached to the other.

As near a long sequester'd vale I drew,
Two seeming strangers started to my view;
Who both appear'd on hostile measures bent,
And soon adjusted their polemic tent:
And thus began——

POLITENESS.
Thy rustic manners and unpolish'd gait,
Thy awkward breeding I entirely hate;
From what religious or sectarian tribe,
Didst thou that blunt rusticity imbibe?
I'll ne'er associate with thy sect I fear,
If I must such an uncouth visage wear.

PIETY.
Of such invectives be not so profuse,
Tho' I your wild unmeaning cants disuse:
Your chiefest aim is how an artful wile
May gain you friendship by a flatt'ring smile;
Your whole affections and deluded mind,
To Fops and Fashions chiefly are confin'd.

POLITENESS.
For what design was ever man ordain'd,
But to live happy and secure a friend?
And such companions still with him unite,
Who's chearful, courtly, affable, polite;
I always have, and shall for evermore,
A humdrum clownish hypocrite abhor.

PIETY.
Delusive thought! 'tis pregnant with mischief!
Fatal thy views! destructive thy belief!
For man was made to aim a nobler prize;
To live for heav'n, and dwell beyond the skies:

To scorn the trappings of the empty fool,
And turn his modish airs to ridicule.
Your courtly manners and attractive smile,
Your humble servant, and your painted guile,
Fall greatly short to gain the better part,
To mend your morals or improve your heart.
Unfeigned friendship is by you forgot;
You deal around your compliments by rote:
The peer, the padler, peasant, or the prince,
Alike are dun'd with your impertinence.

POLITENESS.

For all your pother 'bout religion's cause,
Its moral maxims and eternal laws:
You miss the only and effectual way
To gain the young, the thoughtless, and the gay:
For all your zeal to make a profylete,
You'd make more converts were you more po-
   lite.

PIETY.

Were you as careful to maintain aright,
Your life and conduct in your Maker's sight,
As you appear in fashion to excel,
And rival ev'ry modern beau and belle:
Their splendid flatt'ry you would soon deride,
And all such gilded tinsel lay side.
But ah! my friend, with what unwearied toil
Do you your neighbours and yourself beguile.
Remote from each your thoughts and words are
   plac'd,
Politeness by Profaneness is defac'd.

POLITENESS.

How could I with your brotherhood engage,
At once the scorn and pity of our age?
Last night at Madam Modish festive board,
What laughter did your cynic whims afford:
By ev'ry member you were stigmatiz'd,
And for your conduct mortally despis'd:
With this suggestion each of them confide,
" That you have less humility than pride."
You plume yourself, I fear, to more excess,
On your reserve, than foplings on their dress:
Your manner's so uncourtly and severe,
You wear the touchy aspect of a bear.
Now as I'm not ambitious for disgrace,
In ev'ry corner where I set my face,
I'll still those sing'lar oddities of thine,
With studious care in ev'ry place decline.

PIETY.

When I've beheld your artificial smile,
Your proffer'd service, and your friendly stile;
Your readiness to soothe the mind of woe,
And for your neighbour ev'ry thing forego:
When I beheld, at once, display'd in thee,
Vivacious humour and urbanity;
A heart to friendship seemingly inclin'd,
Improv'd by labour, and by art refin'd;
An anxious wish your ev'ry friend to please,
Whether attain'd by labour or by ease;
Ransacking ev'ry corner of your mind,
Where you the most attractive words might find;

With

With studious care arranging ev'ry phrase,
And more afraid of evil words than ways;
Acquaint with all the modes of spacious guile,
" Or the cheap friendship of a flatt'ring smile;"
Your graceful mien, I own, I have admir'd,
And wish'd, at times, I were with it inspir'd.
But ah! should one, unmindful of his fame,
Your Maker's precepts or religion name,
No more your gay attractive smiles appear;
His serious strain is hooted with a sneer:
Vivacity then flies—and in its room
There sits a pensive or a sullen gloom.
And when united with the sportive crew,
Where each companion's full as bad as you,
Your conduct there appears entirely plain,
To man *polite*, to God alone *profane*.

POLITENESS.

Such spurious logic I may fitly call,
" A barrel thrown out to amuse the *Whale:*"
As sailors do, that they may safely slip
That monster's jaws with their endanger'd ship.
Before your face, your neighbour's faults, I find,
You always place, but screen your own behind.
No charity within your breast remains,
But party-zeal without a rival reigns.
You've learn'd betimes with a malicious frown,
To view each tribe and party but your own.
And those in whom the flames of hatred burn,
With equal rage your compliment return.

Moſt of your prieſts to endleſs woe condemn
All thoſe who ſay not Shibboleth* like them;
And more reſent an error in the mind,
Than vices of the moſt flagicious kind.
Of either tribe I'll ne'er a member be,
Who with each other never can agree.

PIETY.

If mortal man had nothing elſe to fear,
But human ſcorn and reſentment here :
Did each of us, as the brute creation muſt,
For ever mingle with our ancient duſt :
Had he, who at the firſt our being gave,
Ne'er fir'd our hopes with life beyond the grave:
Had virtue ne'er been made the only teſt,
By which immortal ſpirits can be bleſt ;
Then might we ſafely all our views confine,
To modes and manners, friends and gen'rous wine,
But ah! to man a greater taſk is giv'n,
T' improve the ſoul, and mould it fit for heav'n.
Since it is ſo, our ſwift departing hours
Demand th' exertion of our utmoſt pow'rs;
T' obey our Creator, and our conſcience right,
Of greater moment than to be polite.

POLITENESS.

But I could mention ſeveral friends of mine,
Whoſe hearts to virtue ſecretly incline ;
Their Maker's judgments and his precepts fear,
Eſteem his worſhip, and his laws revere;
Who bluſh, with conſcious ſhame in your behalf,
While ſatire dubs you, an untuttor'd calf;

* A military watch-word uſed by the Gileadites.—
See Judges xii. 6.

Unknown

Unknown to virtues of the social kind,
A generous soul, or sentiment refin'd.
Detested always in your neighbour's sight,
As neither chearful, friendly, nor polite.

   When youthful minds hear virtue thus arraign'd,
And by your carriage wantonly disdain'd;
A path reverse their eager steps pursue,
And early bid religious thoughts adieu.
They dread the scorn of each licentious knave,
And shrink at slander more than at the grave.
They choice delib'rately of either two,
Eternal vengeance than be laugh'd at now:
Adjudging him, of all, the most forlorn,
Who for religion daily suffers scorn:
Whose name is toss'd with contempt thro' the town,
By ev'ry wit'ling, blackguard, or buffoon.
Of various stigmas you're the fatal cause,
Which vice exulting o'er religion draws:
To these effects your rustic manners tend,
And only wound the cause they should defend.
Your rigid maxims men will still despise,
While *virtue's* drest in such pedantic guise!

PIETY.

Would you adopt the antiquated mode,
" To join politeness with the fear of God;"
When you devote as many hours to pray'r
As *Strap* consumes in dressing of your hair.
Without reluctance I'll adopt the plan,
And blend politeness with the pious man:
But while so many graceless fops I see,
Like fire and water we will ne'er agree.

OCCASIONAL

OCCASIONAL REFLECTIONS.

With much regret, the muse has long beheld
These mighty rivals with resentment steel'd;
With jealous eye each counteracts the plan
Which his opponent studiously began:
Each views his neighbour's conduct with disdain,
And attributes it to a troubled brain;
With how much freedom might they both unite,
For each opponent's partly in the right;
But dust of prejudice inflames their eyes,
What both should love, they mutually despise.
Ah! could the muse insep'rably unite,
In mutual league the pious and polite;
While they're dismember'd, mortals never can
Behold a perfect well accomplish'd man.
In vain we strive to emulate the mode,
While we're defective in our love to God;
Nor can our system ever be divine,
Till candid elegance our thoughts refine.
Yet *Fops of fashion*, full of courtly stile,
Explode religion with a haughty smile;
While *rustic virtue* think'st a sin to join
Accomplish'd breeding with the laws divine.
Repugnant paths they eagerly pursue,
Each has a diff'rent object in his view.
Averse to each as much as mortals can;
One feareth *God*, another only *man*.
They 'fend the truth with much perswasive art,
Yet each of them contends but for a part.
Would Virtue and Politeness only join,
The lovely union would appear divine.

Ah!

Ah! could the muse with success interpose,
In peace unite these irritated foes.
Were not her feeble council ta'en amiss,
Her admonition would be plainly thus:—
Let *rustic virtue* meet with open arms,
Politeness drest in all its finest charms;
And none assume to imitate the *mode*
Who does not truly fear Almighty God;
Nor none of them be so intently prone,
To blame his neighbour's faults, as mend his own:
Detest the noise of such polemic thunder,
And once UNITED ne'er divide ASUNDER!

The Creed Versified.

*ONE God supreme I firm believe to be,
Who is, and was, from all eternity;
Almighty Creator of unbounded space,
Father of me, and all the human race:
And in Messiah, God's eternal Son,
Who was conceived in a virgin's womb,
Thro' pow'r supernal of the Holy Spirit,
And by his blood did our redemption merit;
Who was by Pilate's self-condemn'd decree,
With cruel hands nail'd to the shameful tree:
For our offences bow'd his sacred head,
And dwelt within the chambers of the dead.
But from the grave the third day he arose,
Triumphing over death, and all his foes.
And when his mission here on earth did end,
To God the Father did at last ascend:
Enthron'd on high, he sits at God's right hand,
While heav'n and earth are under his command:

From

From thence, as Judge, he will at laſt come down,
When quick and dead ſhall have their final doom.
I do believe there is a Holy Ghoſt,
(A triune God is ſtill my hope and boaſt:)
That ſaints on earth do in communion live :
That God, thro' Jeſus, will our ſins forgive :
And that our bodies from the duſt ſhall riſe :
And in eternal life that never dies.

A SOLILOQUY.
Written in a Country Church yard.

STRUCK with religious awe and ſolemn dread,
I view theſe gloomy manſions of the dead.
Around me tombs in mixt diſorder riſe,
And in mute language teach me to be wiſe.
Time was, theſe aſhes liv'd—a time muſt be
When others thus may ſtand—and look at me ;
Alarming thought! no wonder 'tis we dread
O'er theſe uncomfortable vaults to tread;
Where blended lie the aged and the young,
The rich and poor, an undiſtinguiſh'd throng :
Death conquers all, and time's ſubduing hand
Nor tombs nor marble ſtatues can withſtand.

Mark yonder aſhes in confuſion ſpread!
Compare earth's living tenants with her dead!
How ſtriking the reſemblance, yet how juſt!
Once life and ſoul inform'd this maſs of duſt ;
Around theſe bones, now broken and decay'd,
The ſtreams of life in various channels play'd :
Perhaps that ſkull, ſo horrible to view,
Was ſome fair maid's, ye belles, as fair as you;

Theſe

These hollow sockets two bright orbs contain'd,
Where the loves sported, and in triumph reign'd;
Here glow'd the lips; there. white as Parian stone,
The teeth, dispos'd in beauteous order shone.
This is life's goal—no farther can we view;
Beyond it, all is wonderful and new.
Oh deign! some courteous ghost, to let us know,
What we must shortly be—and you are now!
Sometimes you warn us of approaching fate;
Why hide the knowledge of our present state?
With joy behold us tremblingly explore
Th' unknown gulf, that you can fear no more!
The grave has eloquence—its lectures teach,
In silence, louder than divines can preach:
Hear what it says—ye sons of folly, hear!
It speaks to you—O give it then your ear!
It bids you lay all vanity aside:
O what a lecture this for human pride!

 The clock strikes twelve—how solemn is the sound!
Hark how the strokes from hollow vaults rebound;
They bid us hasten to be wise, and show
How rapid in their course the minutes flow.
See yonder yew—how high it lifts its head!
Around their gloomy shade the branches spread;
Old and decay'd it still remains a grace,
And adds more solemn horror to the place.

 Whose tomb is this? it says, 'tis *Myra's* tomb;
Pluck'd from the world in beauty's fairest bloom:
Attend ye fair! ye thoughtless, and ye gay!
For *Myra* dy'd upon her nuptial day!

The grave, cold bridegroom! clafp'd her in its
    arms,
And the worm rioted upon her charms.
  In yonder tomb the old *Avaro* lies;
Once he was rich—the world efteem'd him wife;
Schemes unaccomplifh'd labour'd in his mind,
And all his thoughts were to the world confin'd;
Death came unlook'd for—from his grafping
    hand,
Down drop'd his bags and mortgages of land.
  Beneath this fculptur'd pompous marble ftone
Lies youthful *Florio*, aged twenty-one;
Cropt like a flow'r, he wither'd in his bloom,
Tho' flatt'ring life had promis'd years to come;
Ye filken fons! ye Florios of the age,
Who tread in giddy maze, life's flow'ry ftage!
Mark here the end of man, in *Florio* fee
What you and all the fons of earth fhall be.
  There, low in duft the vain *Hortenfio* lies,
Whofe fplendour once we view'd with envious
    eyes;
Titles and arms his pompous marble grace,
With a long hift'ry of his noble race:
Still after death his vanity furvives,
And on his tomb all of *Hortenfio* lives.
Around me as I turn my wand'ring eyes,
Unnumber'd graves in awful profpect rife,
Whofe ftones fay only when their owners dy'd,
If young, or aged, and to whom ally'd.
On others pompous epitaphs are fpread,
In mem'ry of the virtues of the dead:
                                            O!

waste of praise, since flatt'ring or sincere,
The judgment-day alone will make appear.
How silent is this little spot of ground!
How melancholy looks each object round!
Here man dissolv'd in shatter'd ruin lies,
So fast asleep—as if no more to rise;
'Tis strange to think how these dead bones can live,
Leap into form, and with new heat revive;
Or how this trodden earth to life shall wake,
Know its old place, its former figure take!
But whence these fears? when the last trumpet sounds
Thro' heav'n's expanse, to earth's remotest bounds,
The dead shall quit these tenements of clay,
And view again the long extinguish'd day:
It must be so—the same Almighty pow'r
From dust who form'd us, can from dust restore.
Cheer'd with this pleasing hope, I safely trust
Jehovah's pow'r to raise me from the dust;
On his unfailing promises rely,
And all the horrors of the grave defy.

The Commandments.—*First Version.*

1. ONE God supreme thou only shalt adore,
2. Nor once the aid of idols e'er implore.
3. Unlawful swearing constantly refrain:
4. The holy Sabbath never do profane.
5. With filial love thy parents honour still;
6. Anger suppress, lest thou thy neighbour kill.

7 All lewd temptations carefully decline,
8 Nor in the least another's right purloin.
9 In witness bearing never speak a lie,
10 Nor yet thy neighbour's happiness envy.

Second Version.

⁎ ONE God there is, supremely great and just.
Him only shalt thou fear, obey, and trust.
2 Nor let another of his glory share,
By making unto idols fruitless pray'r.
3 Ne'er take thy Maker's glorious name in vain,
To be polite, thou must not be profane.
4 With holy rev'rence spend the sabbath day,
Attend on worship, meditate and pray.
5 If thou would'st of his lasting blessings share,
Thy aged parents constantly revere.
6 Suppress thy rage, nor murder ever try,
For murder'd blood does still for vengeance cry.
7 Shun lewd temptations, and the harlot's train,
They are short pleasures, but a lasting pain.
8 Let justice shine thro' all thy actions bright,
Nor in the least invade another's right.
9 Let unbrib'd conscience thy dictator be,
And studiously from perjuration flee.
10 Resign'd to God, and likewise to thy lot,
Thy neighbour's wife, or riches covet not.

The

Third Version.

⁎ ATTEND, O mortal man! behold and see,
No other Gods can be compar'd to me.

2 No sculptur'd image can regard thy cry,
No idol can thy daily wants supply.

3 Vengeance awaits the careless and profane,
Who wantonly express my name in vain.

4 In true devotion, still one day of sev'n,
To God thy maker must be strictly giv'n.

5 Emblems of me, from whom all blessings flow,
Thou to thy parents still must honour shew.

6 Restrain thy passion, nor let anger burn
Within thy breast, lest it to murder turn.

7 Still shun with care the wanton harlot's bed,
To swift destruction all her pleasures lead.

8 Use no deception tho' thy heart incline,
Nor in the least thy neighbour's goods purloin.

9 Let truth within thy lips be daily found,
Nor once another's reputation wound.

10 Tho' on thy neighbour plenty still attends,
Be thou content with what my wisdom sends.

The Lord's Prayer.—*Last Version* *.

⁎ GREAT Parent of the universal frame,
May ev'ry creature love and fear thy
name;

* The different versifications of this inimitable model of Prayer, as well as the three preceding versions of the Decalogue, were chiefly composed by the author with a view to attract the attention of the younger class of his readers; as he humbly conceives they will not be improper lessons for children to commit to memory.

May Satan's kingdom constantly decline,
And on its ruins firm establish thine:
To earth's wide empire let thy grace be giv'n
To do thy will as angels do in heav'n:
From thee, O Lord! supremely great and good,
We ask, and still receive our daily food:
Forgive our long contracted debts, by grace,
As we th' insolvent from the jail release:
Teach us to shun where'er temptation lies,
Whether unmask'd, or yet in secret guise;
And when involv'd in sin, or pain, or grief,
Exert thy pow'r and send us quick relief.
To thee the pow'r and glory do pertain,
As was, and is, and shall be still.   Amen.

. *Second Version.*

ALMIGHTY Father, Lord of earth and heav'n,
May all submission to thy name be giv'n;
Extend thy kingdom, and thy mighty sway;
As those in heav'n, may we on earth obey.
Our mod'rate wants we humbly ask from thee,
" But give us neither wealth nor poverty;"
Forgive, in mercy, all our sins below,
As we forgiveness unto others shew:
Preserve us from temptation ev'ry hour,
Nor leave us to the rage of Satan's pow'r;
For thine's the kingdom, glory, pow'r and praise,
And shall be still, thro' everlasting days.

Third

Third Version.

⁂ FATHER of heav'n and earth supreme,
By whom we move and live;
All rev'rence to thy holy name
May ev'ry creature give.

II.
Extend thy kingdom ev'ry day,
And let thy grace be giv'n,
That saints on earth may thee obey,
As angels do in heav'n.

III.
O thou! whose wisdom understands
Whate'er thy creatures need,
'Tis from thy all-supporting hands,
We seek our daily bread.

IV.
Forgive our sins while here below,
('Tis by thy grace we live)
And still to us such mercy shew,
As we to others give.

V.
That we, 'gainst thee may never sin,
Nor on it set our eyes;
O! let us never come within
The place where evil lies.

VI.
The kingdom, pow'r, and glory's thine,
And shall be ever more:
Let saints and angels still combine,
Thy goodness to adore.

Fourth Version.

⁂ FATHER of all, by heav'n and earth ador'd,
Supremely great, and universal Lord,
Thro' ev'ry age, in ev'ry place, the same.
Be rev'rence paid to thy Almighty name.
May all submissive to thy great command,
On earth below, as saints in heaven stand.
Advance the gracious kingdom of thy Son,
And to his standard let all nations come.
From time to time we on thy grace rely,
Do thou with food our daily wants supply.
Extend thy mercy and our sins remit,
As we, by grace, forgive our neighbour's debt.
From Satan guard our footsteps ev'ry day,
Nor let us yield unto temptation's sway;
For pow'r and glory do belong to thee,
As was, and is, and ever more shall be.

Fifth Version.

⁂ ALMIGHTY Father, Lord of heav'n,
All glory to thy name be giv'n;
Promote the kingdom of thy Son,
And let thy will on earth be done.
Thou source of life, supremely good;
Give us this day our daily food;
And constantly our sins forgive,
As we do those with whom we live.
From evil guard us ev'ry hour;
Nor leave us in temptation's pow'r;
To thee belong, thro' endless day,
The kingdom, glory, and the sway.

₊ *Sixth Version.*

THOU ever gracious universal Sire,
    May filial honour still be paid to thee;
Let all that dwell in heav'n and earth conspire
    To praise thy name in sacred harmony.

II.

May ev'ry nation own thy rightful sway;
    Be just allegiance to thy sceptre giv'n;
Be human mortals careful to obey
    Thy sacred will, as angels do in heav'n.

III.

O thou! to whom the hungry ravens cry,
    From whom the lions daily food implore;
Our needful wants from time to time supply,
    From thy abundant never-fading store.

IV.

May we compassionate our greatest foe,
    In bonds of peace let us united be;
And such forgiveness ev'ry neighbour shew,
    As we expect, impartial Judge, from thee.

V.

Where'er temptations spread their fatal snare,
    And ev'ry luring artifice display,
Do thou conduct, by thy parental care,
    Our footsteps always in the perfect way.

VI.

To the uncreated Majesty of heav'n,
   Who reigns supreme throughout infinite space;
Let ceaseless adoration still be giv'n,
   When time has run its circumscribed race.

An Advice.

⁎⁎⁎ WHOEVER would his reputation save,
And bear it spotless with him to the grave,
Take this *advice* as your prudential guide,
Familiar converse frequently avoid ⁎.
An unreserved man is seldom seen
To hold his neighbour's permanent esteem;
For if familiar converse you indulge,
And then at random all your thoughts divulge;
'Tis ten to one but this shall be your lot,
To be despised as a simple sot.
Thro' too much freedom in your conversation,
You lessen in your neighbour's estimation;
By slow degrees your weakness you disclose,
Till all your foibles ev'ry neighbour knows.
Whatever ignorance you have reveal'd,
You know your silence might have well concceal'd;
For 'tis a maxim both with old and young,
A fool is wise as long's he holds his tongue.

Benevolence.

⁎⁎⁎ WHEN from the source of life I still survey
Jehovah's bounty running ev'ry day;
When I behold his undeserved grace
To me, the worst of all the fallen race;
How great's the debt which I to mercy owe?
Whose gifts to me perpetually flow:

⁎ The author does not here mean to insinuate, either directly or indirectly, that we are to use hypocrisy or yet dissimulation; but only to blend a little of the wisdom of the serpent with the innocence of the dove; which, to every inconsiderate person, must be a seasonable caveat.

Since my returning wants are thus supply'd,
That none for soul nor body are deny'd;
Thy gifts to others freely I'll impart,
Nor unsupply'd let indigence depart;
The hoary head, the blind, the lame, the poor,
In fruitless time shall ne'er attend my door;
For all I give, or get, or do possess,
Come from the Parent of the human race:
Then why should I at all unwilling be
To give to others what God gives to me!

An Estimate of human Happiness.

*** UNNUMBER'D crowds are daily on the road
That leads from grief's to happiness' abode.
With pleasing hope they view the shining prize,
But as they run the gilded phantom flies:
From morn to noon, from youth to age they chace,
With one pursuit, in quest of happiness;
Unpleas'd with past, expecting still to draw
More comfort from the time they never saw:
Strange coz'nage this! that men their thoughts employ
On what they want, and not what they enjoy.

Repentance.

*** A Cloud of guilt's impending o'er my mind,
My soul lock'd up by conscious sin confin'd,
Far from that peaceful quietude of heart,
Which Jesus does to faithful souls impart.
Thou monster sin! thou en'my of my peace!
By thee I'm sunk in sorrow and disgrace.
Ah! foolish self-deceiver that I've been,

Whose

Whose blinded eyes, till now, have never seen
That dreadful precipice of ruin's brink,
From which my guilty soul did almost sink
Into that gulf where demons must remain,
By God's decree consign'd to endless pain.
O! were my soul at last from sin set free;
How glad, how thankful, would my spirit be!
With heart exulting, and with songs of praise,
I'd rest in peace, and spend my waiting days.
Until made meet for happiness divine,
Then should I cheerfully my breath resign,
And land at last on heav'n's eternal shore,
Where sin, and grief, and pain, are felt no more.

A Thought on Sickness.

WHEN growing sickness still increase the fears,
And death with all his fatal train appears,
By turns the senses wishfully incline,
To have the lawyer, surgeon, and divine:
Nor ease, nor comfort from the nearest friend;
Strangers, unwelcome visitants, offend;
And while in vain he panteth after ease,
The most attentive servant cannot please.
Conversing tires him, to be silent grieves;
That all are foes he frequently believes.
Wishful to know of ev'ry one their mind,
Whether he be for life or death design'd;
With ghastly looks he stares you in the face,
Impatient, asks your thoughts about his case.
His former vices, join'd to present care,
With poignant darts still drive him to despair;

Anxious

Anxious to find a cordial for his pain,
For help he cries, but still he cries in vain.
His titles, riches, dignity and pow'r,
How vain, how useless, in this awful hour.
Ye, who enjoy your health and active pow'rs,
What's his to day, to-morrow may be yours.

Contentment.

. OF all the blessings men enjoy below,
Contentment is the greatest that we know;
For ev'ry man, in ev'ry age and clime,
Esteems *contentment* as a thing divine.
To find it out *ambition* for his guide
Takes with him fame, with self-esteem and pride;
While *av'rice* cries he's frequently been told,
Contentment lies in hoarded bags of gold;
Ebriety declares, *contentment* joins
Itself to those who quaff the richest wines;
Learning maintains 'tis with the studious sage,
Who for *contentment* hunts the folio page.

Thus, ev'ry ruling passion more or less,
Is still pursuing after happiness;
While each regrets that all their labours tend
To baulk their expectations in the end.

But he that wants to find this hidden prize,
Must search the chamber where true virtue lies;
'Tis there *contentment* makes its chief abode;
The way to virtue is the way to God!

Avarice and Ambition.

. TO live above your station plainly shews
How far your proud and haughty spirit
 goes;

To

To live below it, shews a narrow mind;
Therefore avoid extremes of ev'ry kind.

Envy and Detraction.

**ESTEEM and merit libertines envy,
But never tread the path in which they lie;
When men despair to raise their worth or fame,
'Tis then they try to blast another's name.
For none eyes merit with a peevish frown,
But such as have no merit of their own.

The Life of Pleasure.

LIVE while you live, the Epicure will say,
And take the pleasures of the present day:
Live while you live, the sacred prophet cries,
And give to God each moment as it flies.
Lord, in my view, let both united be;
I live in *pleasure* when I *live* to thee!

Anger and Revenge.

**WHEN folly blows the flames of anger fast,
Sure in repentance anger ends at last;
For if your passion you can ne'er subdue,
Remember passion soon will vanquish you.
When men in quarrels frequently engage,
What reason wants they make it up in rage;
Revengeful anger no restriction knows,
Strokes follow words, and murder follows blows.
Therefore let mildness in your carriage shine;
To err is human; to forgive divine!

Education.

**THIS is the best employ a man can find,
To rule his passions and improve his mind;
'Twas

'Twas rightly judged of an ancient sage *,
Who bade youth *learn* what they should *do* in age;
For this is learning's ultimate design
That *wit* and *virtue* in our hearts might join;
Whoe'er attends not to this golden rule
Is either vicious, or a sottish fool.

Cruelty and Oppression.

*.*OUR virtue, truth, and spotless innocence,
Against tyrannic pow'r are no defence;
If force and malice shall their pow'r unite,
When they accuse, their accusation's right.
Force rules the world, and bends and breaks its laws,
And makes the worst an equitable cause;
In fruitless toil for Justice we pursue,
While our opponent's Judge and party too.
Our laws (as spider's webs the flies enthral)
Oft catch the light, but let the weighty fall,
In vain the *lamb* enjoys the better cause,
While still the *wolf* retains the strongest paws.

The Grave.

.'TIS here the fool, the wise, the low, the high,
In mix'd disorder and in silence lie;
Here kings and statesmen unregarded dwell;
Forget their stations in this gloomy cell.
The mighty prince who never saw his peer,
O'ercome by death, has made his chamber here;
We saw of late his high aspiring mind,
To vast dominions could not be confin'd;

* Agesilaus.

Yet here, alas! he seeks his last retreat;
Resigns the pomp and splendour of the great.
The gen'ral that in triumph left the field
Did here, to death, his life and honours yield.
O mighty death! who can thy pow'r outbrave,
When kings lie vanquish'd in this silent grave?
If in their stead a vassal might suffice,
Their names and honours would immortalize:
Could warlike bands cause thee to disappear,
Sure these great men would never have come here.
'Tis here all ranks in equal balance poize,
For with the master, here the servant lies.
O! humbling thought, must pride be thus disgrac'd;
Are all distinctions here at last effac'd?

In this dark cavern lies a hoary head,
That long has wish'd to number with the dead
'Tis now his sickness and his sorrows end;
In death he found his best and only friend:
No more beneath life's weighty load he goes,
But in this chamber finds a quiet repose.

Here with the aged lies a lovely boy,
His father's darling, and his mother's joy:
Yet death, regardless of the parent's tears,
Snatch'd him away while in the bloom of years;
With mournful hearts the rueful way they tread,
And leave their child within this silent bed.

Lo! here the gay, the fam'd *Miranda* lies,
On whom of late each gallant fix'd his eyes,
That lovely frame, so much its owner's boast,
Is in this *grave* thro' putrefaction lost.
Ye airy prudes, who still yourselves adore,
The gay *Miranda*'s beauty is no more.

Here

Here lies the *Hector*, whose unrivall'd strength
The wasting hand of time cut down at length;
Who death nor danger never once did fear,
Crush'd by the feeble moth lies mould'ring here.
  Lucretta here among this dust I find,
Whose late contracted and penurious mind,
Unmov'd by indigence or sorrow's cry,
Did still his aid to helpless want deny:
Who as a factor for his thriftless heir,
A vast extensive fortune did prepare:
Behold the wild, the thoughtless youth rejoice,
When death in silence clos'd his father's eyes:
How would *Lucretta's* peevish heart be pain'd,
To see such waste of what he dearly gain'd.
Here in this grave *Lucretta* I behold,
Depriv'd of all his hoarded bags of gold.
  While bending o'er this venerable urn,
My thoughts towards my dissolution turn:
The fatal hour is fast approaching nigh,
When I with these shall undistinguish'd lie.
O! thou who rose triumphant o'er the grave,
My soul in that important moment save;
When I deposite here this mortal clay,
Receive my soul to everlasting day!

The vision. Job iv. 12,—21.

'TWAS at the dark and silent hour of night,
    When airy visions skim before the sight;
When men entranc'd in balmy sleep are laid,
And deeper slumbers ev'ry sense invade;
A voice, shrill sounding, pierc'd my list'ning ear,
The solemn accent still methinks I hear.

And lo! arose before my wond'ring eyes,
A shapeless spectre of stupendous size;
Sullen, it me approach'd with awful grace,
And frowning dreadful star'd me in the face.
Deep sunk my heart, my hair erected stood,
And sweaty drops my shaking limbs bedew'd.
At length a voice the solemn silence broke,
And thus, in hollow tone, the phantom spoke:
What art thou, mortal man, thou breathing clod?
Thou daring rival of thy author God?
Is then this heap of animated dust
Pure as his maker? as his maker just?
What are the gifts to human nature giv'n,
That man usurps the attributes of heav'n?
Th' angelic hosts that on the Godhead wait,
And issue forth his ministers of fate;
Not of themselves perform his great command,
But on his guidance and o'er-ruling hand.
Shall then presumptous man his actions sway,
This lordly tenant of a lump of clay?
Who from a sordid mass derives his birth,
And drops again into his mother earth;
Whose carcase moul'dring in the silent tomb,
Devouring reptiles mangle and consume.
Look round the surface of this earthly ball,
See grandeur vanish, and ev'n nations fall!
What millions die, the race of being run,
Between the rising and the setting sun!
See man each hour resign his fleeting breath,
And sink unheaded in the jaws of death!
Thus falls thy boasted wisdom, mortal man,
A cloud its substance, and its date a span!

Thy

Thy short perfection on thy life depends;
At death's great period all thy knowledge ends.

Rash Judgment.

⁎ WHAT numbers rashly judge before they
try,
They hate the man and yet they know not why;
Without e'er knowing if there's greater cause,
For rigid censure than for just applause.
We pin our faith unto our neighbour's sleeves,
What rashness says, credulity believes.
When our aversion springs from such a spirit,
How often falls it on the man of merit.
If glaring facts at last the truth unfold,
We blush to own the fictions we have told.
No right excuse for this can we advance,
But only blame our own precipitance.

Contentment.

⁎ IF thoughtless man could only reason right,
And view each object in its proper light;
If, with compassion, we would trouble eye
As often as we happiness envy,
Imaginary wants would be forgot,
And all would be contented with their lot.

Divine Power.

⁎ WHEN roaring tempests all their forcestry;
With tossing billows mounting to the sky,
Thy mighty voice reclaims their swelling pride,
And calms the surges of the foaming tide.
The tempest dies upon the peaceful shore;
At thy command its waves are heard no more.

The clouds and skies obey thy sov'reign will,
And from their bottles all our rivers fill:
Impell'd by thy command, their fatness pours
On ev'ry herb and field in balmy show'rs:
The wand'ring clouds, the hail, the feather'd snow,
Thy boundless pow'r and wisdom plainly show.

Hope.

⁎ WHAT tho' misfortune clouds our mental joys,
While fleeting here, our peace of mind destroys:
Inspiring hope recruits our languid mind
Of future rest, when here no more confin'd;
Amidst the gloomy shades of midnight grief,
These expectations chear with fresh relief;
Such hopes expel our fear when once begun,
As noxious damps before the rising sun:
This day our spirits, if deprest with sorrow,
Must rest in hope, expecting ease to-morrow;
If we next day should no relief obtain,
We must renew our hope and trust again.
Thus, weath'ring out the tempest's raging tide,
With patient hope in Jesus still confide;
Whose word and pow'r do mutually engage,
To clothe's with strength, or else our grief assuage;
If thus the Lord our patience fortify,
Then death, and grief, and pain, we may defy:
We're here like ships by raging tempests toss'd,
While on our passage to th' eternal coast:
But sov'reign pow'r conducts the tossing helm,
And guides our souls beyond affliction's harm;
Such pregnant hopes our feeble minds sustain,
Till we at last the heav'nly prize attain:

Then

Then faith will end in never fading fight,
And hope be loft in permanent delight.

Universal Praise.

TO thee, Almighty fov'reign of the fkies,
Our loudeft praife in grateful accents rife.
To thee, O fource of life! the earth's whole frame,
Proclaim in higheft ftrains immortal fame:
Thy faints above their heav'nly pow'rs exert,
And in thy praifes bear a chearful part:
The holy prophets join this heav'nly choir,
While faithful martyrs in the fong confpire;
All nature tunes her fweeteft notes to thee,
And founds her voice in facred harmony.
Preferve, O Lord, and daily guide our ways,
Thro' ev'ry period of our wafting days;
Protect our fouls this day from ev'ry ill,
And may thy word and grace our fpirits fill;
At laft receive us to the bleft above,
To praife, with them, thy everlafting love.

Universal Praise to God.

AWAKE my foul, thy grateful tribute bring,
Proclaim the praife of heav'n's eternal King,
Whofe boundlefs love, thro' boundlefs fpace, appears
In ev'ry feafon of the rolling years.
Where-e'er I turn thefe wand'ring thoughts of mine,
Thy pow'r, thy wifdom, and thy goodnefs fhine;
Thro' all the concave of the ftarry fkies
Thy wifdom fhines before my ravifh'd eyes.

The winds confess thy universal sway;
The night proclaims thy glory to the day;
The waves and seas thy mighty pow'r extol,
And loudly sound thy praise from pole to pole;
The frost, the rain, the hail, the feather'd snow,
(These faithful servants of thy will below,)
Proclaim thy glory as they quickly fly
Thro' earth's wide empire from the lofty sky;
The plumy tribes, those tenants of the air,
To thee a song of grateful thanks prepare.
To thee the savage monsters of the wood
Pay thankful homage for their daily food:
Yea ev'ry mouth's a trumpet for thy fame,
To sound the praise of thine eternal name;
Be this my chief, my ultimate desire,
That mine still mingle with that blessed choir.

Common Swearing.

*** A COMMON swearer tells his neighbour plain,
"To trust my bare assertion would be vain;
My simple word's incredible I fear,
No man believes me if I do not swear:
While your mere word establishes a truth,
Mine costs me still the sanction of an oath."
In vain you reason with a swearing fool,
But turn his thoughtless oaths to ridicule.
From common oaths my neighbours to affright,
I only say that phrase is unpolite;
And still I hold it as a maxim clear,
A common swearer is a common liar!

Compassion.

Compassion.

PITY the sorrows of a poor old man,
  Whose trembling limbs have borne him to your door,
Whose days are dwindled to the shortest span,
  Oh! give relief, and heav'n will bless your store,

II.
These tatter'd cloaths my poverty bespeak,
  Those hoary locks proclaim my lengthen'd years;
And many a furrow in my grief-worn cheek
  Has been the channel to a flood of tears.

III.
Yon house erected on the rising ground,
  With tempting aspect drew me from my road;
For plenty there a residence has found,
  And grandeur a magnificent abode.

IV.
Hard is the fate of the infirm and poor!
  Here as I crav'd a morsel of their bread,
A pamper'd menial drove me from the door
  To seek a shelter in a humbler shade.

V.
Oh! take me to your hospitable dome;
  Keen blows the wind, and piercing is the cold!
Short is my passage to the friendly tomb,
  For I am poor, and miserably old.

VI.
Should I reveal the sources of my grief,
  If soft humanity e'er touch'd your breast,
Your hands would not with-hold the kind relief,
  And tears of pity would not be represt.

VI. Heav'n

VII.

Heav'n sends misfortunes; why should we re-
   pine?
  'Tis heav'n has brought me to the state you see;
And your condition may be soon like mine,
  The child of sorrow and of misery.

VIII.

A little farm was my parental lot,
  Then like the lark I sprightly hail'd the morn;
But ah! oppression forc'd me from my cot,
  My cattle died, and blighted was my corn.

IX.

My daughter, once the comfort of my age,
  Lur'd by a villain from her native home,
Is cast abandon'd on the world's wide stage,
  And doom'd in scanty poverty to roam.

X.

My tender wife, sweet smoother of my care,
  Struck with sad anguish at the stern decree,
Fell, ling'ring fell, a victim to despair,
  And left the world to wretchedness and me.

XI.

Pity the sorrows of a poor old man,
  Whose trembling limbs have borne him to your
   door,
Whose days are dwindled to the shortest span,
  Oh! give relief, and heav'n will bless your store.

Company.

*** WHEN from the noisy croud I am re-
   tir'd,
And with my book and meditation fir'd;

                                            When

When no companion rests within my house,
Then self and Satan only can seduce.
But when with man I frequently converse,
My snares and dangers commonly increase:
'Tis plainly clear to the observing eyes,
Snares with companions almost fall and rise.

Jesus weeping over Lazarus' grave.

SEE matchless love in sacred torrents shine,
And fun'ral honours paid with drops divine.

Truth and Dissimulation.

. TRUTH always is consistent with the mind,
And ever ready on our lips we find:
Fearless its honest countenance to show,
It frequently drops out before we know.
Whereas a lie still leaves a check behind;
An indication of a guilty mind.
For lies on conscience never will intrude,
While *one* needs *twenty* more to make it good.

" *These shall go away into everlasting Punishment.*"
Matth. xxv. 46.

. THESE now with sorrow leave the judgment-seat,
While each prepares his fearful doom to meet;
Where the wide furnace all its flames display,
Raging impatient for their destin'd prey.
What shrieks are heard amidst the roaring flames,
By force extorted from their rising pains:

While

While all the pow'rs of heav'n againſt them riſe,
Blind to their tears, and deaf to all their cries.
In deep deſpair their trembling eye-balls roll;
Their outward aſpect ſpeaks their anguiſh'd ſoul.
Deſpair and madneſs now begin to riſe,
While ev'ry beam of hope and comfort dies.
There no reſpite, no interval of pain,
Do theſe condemned malefactors gain:
Their endleſs torments all our thoughts tranſcend,
As great in nature, laſting without end:
Stifled in ſmoke and flames they helpleſs lie,
And gnaw their chains thro' everlaſting day.
And as their pain, ſo does their pow'r increaſe,
And panting for, they flee from happineſs.

No aleviation of their pains is giv'n,
No ray of hope from any point of heav'n;
Chain'd in this burning pool to endleſs pain,
By God's decree for ever to remain;
In fruitleſs pray'r they conſtantly implore
The rapid flames to give their burning o'er:
Wiſhing each day they will at laſt expire,
But ever live in everlaſting fire:
Each panting, groaning, ſtill beneath his load,
And fleeing from a ſin-avenging God.
See how their ſmoke and torments ſtill aſcend,
While racking pains increaſe that never end.
If only, when ten thouſand years expire;
It would abate the raging of the fire;
How would that chink of hope their ſouls revive
In expectation of a full reprive.

But

But here, alas! with still increasing pains,
They must abide in everlasting chains.

"—*But the righteous into Life eternal.*"——
Matth. xxv. 46.

THE faithful friends of Jesus now prepare,
His kingdom, sceptre, crown, and joy to share:
Exulting thro' the regions of the sky,
These heirs of glory now in triumph fly;
Ascend on wings of everlasting love,
To take possession of their thrones above;
And as they mount in rapt'rous joy they sing,
While heaven's wide extended porches ring.
Attending Cherubs there rejoicing stand,
Anxious to meet, and hail this welcome band:
While unknown pleasures here in fountains rise
Before their joyful, wond'ring, ravish'd eyes:
Their golden harps with chearful hands they string,
To sound the praise of heav'n's eternal King:
In robes of grandeur and of glory shine,
And bask in beams of endless love divine:
Here from the fount of never ending joy,
They drink the streams of bliss that never cloy.
New scenes of wonder to their eyes appear,
Each former myst'ry is unfolded here.
With songs of praise they bless the happy hour,
Which their souls resign'd to Jesus' pow'r.
The fruits of all their former toil they share,
And a reward for ev'ry fervent pray'r.

Nor pain, nor sickness, e'er approach them here;
No frightful doubting, no tormenting fear:
Far from the pow'r of Satan, death, or sin,
Where no malignant foe can enter in.
Here Jesus wipes away their former tears;
No tenant here a plaintive aspect wears.
Their golden days they constantly employ
In tasting fresh, and still increasing joy.
Still joining with the blest angelic choir,
To laud their King their sacred lips conspire:
No gloomy shades these fearless souls affright,
For darkness there resigns its pow'r to light:
No want, no wish, no hope unsatisfy'd,
No gift, no favour, no request deny'd.
And as their bliss will still increasing be,
It shall endure thro' all eternity.

§ *Infidelity.*

WHO can *believe* that God abhorreth sin,
    And yet regardless persevere therein?
What man *believes* that God's omniscient eyes,
View all his conduct here beneath the skies?
And fearless, still in secret vice delight,
If he can screen it from his neighbour's sight.
Sure such self-blinded mortals have forgot,
That vengeance from his hands will be their lot.
If God be just, and if his word be true,
None serve their *vices* and their *Maker* too!

The

The Song of the Three Children Paraphrased.

O all ye Works of the Lord, &c. praise him!

BEINGS that lifeless being merely have,
 With those that vegetate and yield increase;
Beings to whom your author senses gave,
And you who mind and intellect possess,
 Quit your distinctions of degree and kind,
  Rise, and in sacred raptures all unite,
To praise for ever that eternal mind,
Who daily blesses all with mercies infinite.

II.

O ye Angels of the Lord, &c.

Immortal substances above!
 Princes obedient! Seraphs bright!
For ever burning with exalted love!
Intelligential rays of the great source of light;
 Hosts of the jealous God! etherial bands,
 Who point his thunderbolts as he commands
  Splendid courtiers of the skies,
  Watchful guards of innocence,
Who guide us here, and waft us hence;
 Angels, dependent deities,
Praise him, whose height your sharpest ken transcends,
Whom not the first-born seraph comprehends.

III.
O ye Heavens, &c.

Amazing fabric of the skies!
Arch'd azure roof, thick set with living fires,
   With orbs unnumber'd of unmeasur'd size;
Which human art in vain to view aspires:
Vast amphitheatre of boundless space,
Where worlds of light run their commanded
    race;
In time and measure musically move,
And thro' variety of figures rove;
Yet keep unwearied their unerring ways.
In you your author wrote his awful name
In lasting characters of flame,
In th' universal language, in a hand
Which all may read, all nations understand.
Thro' your wide regions praise to him be giv'n,
Who fix'd his everlasting throne in the empy-
    rean heav'n.

IV.
O ye Waters that be above the Firmament, &c.

Celestial waters, who at God's command,
   Exalted by his Spirit upwards flew,
   Above the firmament's expanded blue,
And left gross ocean and inferior land.
Parent of elements, primeveal cold,
   Who rais'st to fix'd repose and ease;
With pity from your heights behold
   Your little agitated sister seas,
Whose waves now rise, and now subside,
Toss'd by wind, and dash'd by tide.

To whom your stores auxiliary you lent
    The rebel sturdy giant race,
    And giant sins from earth t' efface,
And drown the ancient world, disdaining to repent.
    Then at the rising of a new
    And better offspring, quickly you
Back to your lofty seats obediently withdrew:
    Ye sure foundations of heav'ns proclaim
    Your Maker's ever-during name;
In your still eloquence his praise rehearse,
Who by your staticks pois'd the new made universe.

V.

O all ye Powers of the Lord, &c.

Ye pow'rs of God, to whose vicegerent care
Empires and fates of kings entrusted are,
Ye sev'n distinguish'd Hierarchies, who stand
Nearest the throne in eminent command;
    Ye eyes of ever waking providence,
    Of wonderful effects the cause unseen,
    Disposing trivial intricate events,
    Beyond the wisdom or the strength of men.
    To him perpetual hallelujah sing,
    Who deigns for man your service to employ:
    To the true source of life, the only King,
Who with a word can save, and with a word destroy.

VI.
O ye Sun, &c.

Unexaufted fource of heat,
   Whofe beams the face of nature paint;
Emblem of all that's good or great,
   Or beauteous or beneficent;
Whofe genial parent rays beftow
Life and light on all below;
On whofe revolving golden car of ftate
The hours, and days, and months, and years, in duteous order wait;
   Fair picture of the glorious caufe of all;
   So fair that erring nations proftrate fall,
   And take the copy for th' original.
   From eaft to weft your journey bright,
   Thro' ev'ry climate as you run,
     Blefs the uncreated Light,
   With whom compar'd you are no Sun.

VII.
And Moon, &c.

Silver Queen of dufky fpheres,
   Whofe cooler fire and female light
Day fupply, difpel our fears,
   And gild the horror of the night;
To whofe imperial fceptre bow,
   Stars above and feas below:
Whofe youth can Phœnix-like return
Like her with folar fire you burn,
Like her rife fairer from your urn,
To God unceafing homage pay,
Whofe native and unborrow'd ray

Nor wanes nor changes undergoes,
Nor shade of variation knows;
Who bears alone unbounded sway,
Nor circumscrib'd by night, nor limited by day.

VIII.

O ye Stars of Heaven, &c.

Spangles of gold, night's richest dress,
  When gay in public she appears,
And glittering bright like diamonds numberless,
  Profusely scatter'd on her sable wears.
Huge worlds, yet seeming little points of light,
Whose distance favours and deceives our sight;
Nearer your blaze and heat we could not bear,
 Nor could you mark the seasons of our year.
  Planets, who regularly move,
  Stars superior fix'd above,
  Who lead thro' night the sailor on,
  Sure as the meridian sun,
Bless him from whom your lustre flows,
  Who guides your circling motions ever right;
Your names, your number, and your nature knows,
  Creator, as in pow'r, in knowledge infinite.

IX.

O ye Showers, &c.

Bless God, ye soft descending show'rs
Earth's balm infus'd to close her op'ning veins,
  To hatch the tender infant flow'rs,
To inform with springing life the drooping plains.

In vain Egyptians boast their seven mouth'd
    Nile
Without your help, supplies their little want;
You water ev'ry coast and ev'ry soil,
And rivers of the world yourselves may vaunt.
From pole to pole you carry due supplies,
    Within no narrow brinks confin'd,
Thro' trackless roads you float along the skies,
    Wafted by providential wind;
    Till far fetch'd northern stores allay
    The parching southern heat of day:
    Bless him whose hand unwearied pours
Rich blessings over all his works in never-ceasing
    show'rs.

X.
And Dews, &c.

Ye drizzling mists, whose silent fall
    Wets deeper than the sounding rain,
Whom solar beams together call,
    Whom solar beams dispel again;
Fogs that thick-gathering can defy
And veil the world's all-seeing eye;
And, 'till dispers'd by his victorious ray,
Spread midnight o'er us in the noon of day.
    Praise him, who tho' a little space,
    He seems to hide his radiant face.
    And when we pray, and when we weep,
    An angry silence seems to keep.
After short gloom shines gracious from above,
In beams of mercy, faithfulness, and love.

XI.
O ye Winds of God, &c.

Cool gales, whose healthful show'ry breeze
Wantons 'midst the flow'rs and trees;
And wilder storms, whose fury sends
    Invisible resistless blows,
The mariner's perfidious friends,
    But dreadful and relentless foes.
Impetuous tyrants of the sea and air,
Who navies rack, and deep fix'd forests tear;
Disturbers of the shatter'd universe,
    Loud rolling thunders rapid wings,
Praise him, whose breath, as you the dust disperse,
    Scatters the pride of states, and monarchies of kings.

XII.
O ye Fire, &c.

Pure heav'nly elemental fire,
    Who rests within your proper sphere,
And flames that towards heav'n aspire,
    And rage at being fetter'd here;
Furious when loose, destroying while you shine,
Ordain'd to waste the world by wrath divine.
That awful God your utmost homage claims,
    Ye executioners of milder ire,
Who needs not gross and ministerial flames,
    But is himself provok'd, the most consuming fire.

XIII.

And Heat, &c.

Son of motion, genial heat,
Who motion in your turn beget,
   Vital principle, whence flow
   Our actions, and our passions too,
  Chymist, whose sympathy unites and binds,
  Each kindred part, and severs foreign kinds,
Chief spring of nature's wonderful machine
Who gives to flow'rs the bloom, and leaves the green,
  Fountain of chearful health, to whom belong
  The gay, the fierce, the beauteous, and the strong;
   Without whose vig'rous energy
   This globe of air, and earth, and sea,
  One joyless, useless, lifeless lump would be.
Praise him, by whom preserv'd subsists the whole,
Nor needs a plastick universal soul.

XIV.

O ye Winter, &c.

Winter, long swoon of each decrepid year,
Who chills its veins, and brings its hoary hair,
When stript of ev'ry beauty nature lies
Thrown into pale and dying agonies;
Bless nature's author, whose reviving breath
Makes spring succeed our winter, life our death.

XV. And

XV.
And Summer, &c.

Summer, the year's more manly age,
  Whose pulse beats strongly, boiling high,
Luxuriant, while the dog-star's rage
  Dares with the fiery Zion vie;
When all that breathe within the waters play,
  Gambols on land the blyth fourfooted throng,
Birds chant melodious on the dancing spray
  And gladsome nature echoes to the song.
    Smallest sparks of life are gay,
    Flies and insects sing and play,
      Lately seeming dead revive,
      Now they wake, and now they live.
Blest season! whose returning fruits and flow'rs,
To earth a yearly paradise restores;
Offer to God your earliest fruits, and raise
Trophies and garlands of unfading praise.

XVI.
O ye Dews, &c.

  Gently-falling pearly dew,
  Liquid diamonds of the morn,
Which various glist'ring to the view,
    Pendant from the leaf or thorn;
  The pomp of nature's dress declare,
  And make the morning self more fair;
  Drops that insects feed and plants,
    And when the meal is done,
  No longer useful to their wants
    Shrink from the warmer sun.
(So manna, o'er the desert spread,
Was melted, having Israel fed;)

Dews,

Dews, that oft have longer shin'd
Harden'd by the northern wind,
Like bright, but brittle chrystal seen,
Or silver frosted o'er the green.
Bless God, who deigns his influence t' infuse
Secret refreshing as the silent dews.

XVII.
And Frosts. &c.

Destroying angel, general blast
  Who lay'st our fertile countries waste,
Whose pinch, nor herb nor animal can bear
    Universal forager!
Leanness, whose teeth, like Pharaoh's kine,
    devour
    What plenteous harvest gave before,
    Yet oft with usury repay
    What their first keenness snatch'd away;
The wearied soil impregnate, and prepare
For fuller richer crops th' ensuing year.
Bless him, whose all disposing providence
  Adds bitter physic to our pleasing food,
With good and evil chequers all events,
  T' exalt his glory, and his creature's good,

XVIII.
O ye Frost and Cold, &c.

Shiv'ring ague of the air,
Churlish colony sent forth
From your inhospitable north;
    Rugged companion of a polar bear,
    Cold, whom like a beast of prey
    Oft by fire we chase away;

  Cold, whose fearing breath bereaves
  Hills of trees, and trees of leaves:
Yet, which atone for all the ills you do,
With trees and leaves you sweep diseases too:
  Bless him whose gracious wisdom stores
  The north with fuel and with furs;
(Furs that defensive armour make,
Soft bastions, which your forces cannot shake)
Who for each ill which here on earth we see,
Provides a fitly-suited remedy.

XIX.

O ye Ice, &c.

Ice, who the fluid element can bind,
Protected from its tyrant wind:
In shining fetters, tho' at large confin'd,
  By thee, the finny race immur'd,
  Rest safe from hooks and nets secur'd.
  Encroaching ships are sudden staid.
  That pass the ancient bounds which prudent
    nature made;
  Nor can th' unwilling captives force their way,
  Held faster than by fabled *Remora*:
By thee, weak waves a solid road can form,
And firm as marble stand the winter's storm.
Nor can the icy sea, when most it swells
  With raging tides, its bridge of chrystal shock;
Bless him who turns hard rock to springing
    wells,
  And turns by you soft water into rock.

XX.

And Snow, &c.

Light congeal'd in feather'd show'rs
  Of innocence the emblem bright,
Mantling trees, and fields, and tow'rs,
  Dazzling with a waste of white.
Flakes, that, thick pouring from the low-hung cloud,
  At once both ornament and safety yield
From piercing cold, whose gather'd fleeces shroud
  The tender verdant offspring of the field;
Bless God, who shields his saints from ev'ry harm,
At whose command fire shall not heat, and snow itself shall warm.

XXI.

O ye Nights, &c.

Relict of chaos, melancholy night,
  Night, at whose pencil's touch the colours fade;
Of nature's landscape, vanish'd from our sight,
  The rose and bri'r are equal in the shade.
Night, the world's dark and temporary grave,
Who lays the monarch level with the slave.
  Daily sabbath, made to rest
  Toiling man and weary beast;
A comforter, in whom th' afflicted find
Oblivion of their woes, and indolence of mind.
Praise him whose radiant and all-piercing light
Makes midnight-darkness clear as noon day light.

XXII.

And Days, &c.

Day, univerſal beauty, ray divine,
    Whom none but guilt and falſehood ever fear;
Truth undiſguis'd and ſpotleſs virtue ſhine
    With native luſtre bright when you appear.
        Day, whom gloomy ſorrow flies,
        Pouring eye-ſight on our eyes;
        Mountain, foreſt, ſea, and plain,
        Departed late, return again.
Nature from night's dark priſon forth you call,
Type of the reſurrection general;
        New motion, and new life you give
        To all that move, and all that live.
Bleſs God, Father of lights, who bids you riſe
With undiſtinguiſh'd beams on friends and ene-
    mies.

XXIII.

O ye Light, &c.

    Light, creation's firſt eſſay,
    Gladſome uſher of the day,
    Who your ſhining parent ſun
    Still attend, and ſtill outrun;
    Pureſt angel's bleſt abode,
    Robe majeſtical of God;
Swifter than whirlwind from the eaſt you flow,
And in an inſtant ſtrike our eyes below;
Who dar'ſt almoſt for ſpeed with ſpirit vie,
For thought, and only thought, can quicker fly.

Whose beams with false unreal colours cheat,
Yet hating falsehood shew your own deceit.
 Whom noblest painter's mimic pain,
 Strives to imitate in vain,
Contracting largest objects, earth or sky,
Within the narrow pupil of the eye:
Praise never-ceasing be to him convey'd,
To whom your utmost lustre's but a shade.

XXIV.

And Darkness, &c.

Darkness, whose empire no beginning knew,
The blind confusion, whence this order grew,
Ere yet the spirit's wings that brooding lay
Had hatch'd the new made world, ere shone the
  joyous day;
 Black privation, shadowy name,
  Phantom, to scare the wicked sent,
 The close retreat of blushing shame,
  Of guilty sin the punishment;
 Dreaded unsubstantial spright,
 Shy vanishing at morning light;
Bless him, whose fertile word to being brought
Light from thy bosom, and the world from nought.

XXV.

O ye Lightenings,

 Rolling thunders, voice divine,
 Light'nings blasting while ye shine,
Th' alarm of angry heav'n, whose terrors make
The nations tremble, and the forests shake;
        God's

God's weapons of resistless flame,
Arrows of sure unerring aim.
Walls within walls no more the passage bar
Than unopposing space of liquid air;
Thro' the welkin see they glide,
Quick to punish human pride.
By these did Sodom's lust in flames expire,
And felt the vengeance of ethereal fire.
Swift-wing'd light'nings, thunders loud,
Praise the everlasting God,
From whom descending at the judgment-day,
Both earth and heav'n itself shall flee away.

XXVI.
And Clouds, &c.

Clouds, soft furls of folded air,
Beauteous tap'stry of the skies;
Ever-fleeting landscapes fair,
With infinite varieties;
Ye pencil lakes, that arm our floods with rage,
God's magazines, when purpos'd war to wage;
Whether to cause the plowman's hopes to fail,
He pours unkindly rain incessant down,
Or else from frozen stores of moulded hail,
Destroy the herbage with a show'r of stone;
Praise him, who, when of old the heav'n's he bow'd,
Choose for his pompous car an awful cloud.
Who, when delighted to appear,
The object more of love than fear,
Assum'd a gentler cloud and milder ray,
To lead his Israel thro' the desart way,
Or o'er the mercy-seat his glory bright display.

XXVII.

O let the Earth bless,
Mother of all things, earth, the womb
Of worms and monarchs, and their tomb;
The happy seat at first of peace.
  Of love, and innocence, and joys;
Untill'd producing blest increase,
  Flowers and fruits of paradise.
Till curs'd for sin, tho' till'd you scarcely grant
Supplies for guilty man's redoubled want;
And yield for chearing wine and strength'ning corn,
The prickly thistle, and the fruitless thorn.
Great theatre of change whereon we play,
  Perhaps a gay, but short and anxious part,
Where sins, vexations, losses, pains allay
  Our greatest joys with sure-attending smart.
    Bless God, and thankfully receive
    What still his goodness deigns to give;
Who grants, when waken'd from your dust we rise,
A better earth, and safer paradise;
Where neither pain nor trouble shall molest,
Nor sin, nor serpent, break our endless rest.

XXVIII.

O ye Mountains,
Mountains, who clouds beneath you can despise,
  Earth's pillars, who triumphant arches form;
  Unshaken objects of perpetual storm;
Beauteous tho' vast, noble deformities:

Old

Old stately monuments of nature's birth,
  Whether you overlook the sea,
  And point to mariners their way;
Or else with various gifts enrich the earth,
Ripen the minerals, and gems, and ore,
And wealthy rivers unexhausted pour;
Fix'd land-marks, friendly umpires of debates,
Ramparts of wars, and boundaries of states;
Bless him who makes your pride to fail,
  Whose presence, when provok'd, you fly,
Lighter than dust within his scale,
  Less than nothing in his eye.

XXIX.

And Hills.

Small hills, whose gently rising height
  And prospects, sweet and pleasant shades;
The pomp of courts and croud of cities flight,
  Thrones of delight, which treason ne'er invades;
Where artless bliss and genuine beauties grow,
That neither av'rice base nor worse ambition know;
Where flocks and herds are shelter'd and are fed,
A table plenteous, and a flow'ry bed;
Praise him, who makes ev'n kings who sceptres
    wield
Dependent on the slighted field,
  With cares and dangers has beset
  The lofty stations of the great;
While calm and safe the middle seats appear
Too high to envy, and too low to fear.

XXX.

XXX.

O all ye Green Things upon the Earth, &c.

Tall stately cedars, sheding rich perfumes,
   Wherewith our verdant Lebanon is grac'd,
Who, self-embalm'd in your own fragrant gums,
   Defy correction, and for ever last.
All that each diff'rent clime or season bears,
Who spicy odours breathe, or balmy tears;
All that from mother earth's fair bosom rise,
Whate'er was known of old to Solomon the wise;
   Or flow'rs our dainty sense to please,
     Or herbs to yield our hunger food,
   Simple to remedy disease,
     To temper or exalt our blood;
Bless him, who gave you virtues and your scents,
Whose hand your various glowing colours paints;
Colours whose native lustre has outshone
Great *David's* pompous heir, bright on his iv'ry
   throne.

XXXI.

O ye Wells bless, &c.

Fountains, transparent mirrors, where
'The sun delighted to appear,
Stamps on fluid trembling glass
His glorious tho' reflected face;
Common, yet precious vessels which o'erflow,
And silver, potable on all bestow;
Praise him, who feeds your springs, and want
   supplies;
The never failing source, whence living waters
   rise.

XXXII.

O ye Seas,

Monster, whose foam and roaring threat the shore;
   Who, like a lion couchant in the way,
   Sometimes with seeming sleep deceive your prey;
Then sudden rous'd insatiably devour.
Yet made a beast of burden ye convey
Treasures of diff'rent coasts along the wat'ry way.
The-strong like Sampson's riddle yielding sweet,
The great devourer thus affording meat.
Praise him, whose nod presiding o'er the deep,
Or swells to storms, or bids the ocean sleep,
Fast bound by his Almighty hand
In adamantine chains of despicable sand.

XXXIII.

And Floods, &c.

Rivers, earth's circulating blood,
   Which feeds her seas, and feeds her lands;
The life of inland trade, whose friendly flood
   Far distant cities joins in sure tho' fluid bands;
Serpentine waters who yourselves outrun,
   Yet with an equal space yourselves pursue;
Your mansions always keep and always shun,
   Ever the same, yet ever new.
     Useful wanderers that err
     Your blessings wider to confer,
Ceaseless exalt his praise, from whom alone
Created beings flow, himself deriv'd from none.

XXXIV.

O ye Whales, and all that move in the Waters, &c.

Ye whales, who midst the wide extended main,
    When floating huge-like living islands show,
Where lawless tyrants uncontroul'd you reign,
    And fat with lives of your inferiors grow.
    Who sport at large, and take your ease
    In spacious azure palaces:
Whose boding visits from afar,
No less than earthquakes, or a bearded star;
Your conscious brother tyrants fear,
And by your ruin dread their own is near.
Ye lesser sea-born nations, nameless fry,
Who by uncounted millions multiply;
Ye curious work of sporting nature's hand,
Who imitate each species of the-land.
Strangers to sound, your Maker's glory raise,
And let your silence speak aloud his praise.

XXXV.

O all ye Fowls of the Air, &c.

    Inhabitants of wood and air,
      With rich embroider'd plumage fair;
Builders, whose structures far transcend
    What human architecture shows;
Of diff'rent form, yet all defend
    The callow breed from cold and foes.
Wise prophets of the future year,
    Who fly from mischiefs ye forsee;
Poetic choirs, who charm the ear
    With artless melting melody.

                                        Nature

Nature compoſing ev'ry ſong
   Echo'd to the dales and groves,
Wherein the painted feather'd throng
   Sing their paſſions and their loves.
To God, who gave your ſweeteſt lays,
Grateful chant ye hymns of praiſe.

XXXVI.
O all ye Beaſts and Cattle, &c.

Brutes, grov'ling ſpirits, ſouls that die,
   Slaves to your ſenſes and to man:
Oft ſhewing when you fight or fly,
   His forfeited dominion vain.
Living machines, by art divine,
   Built beyond deſcription fine;
Purſuing nature's end, by inſtinct taught,
Whoſe ſtrange impulſes oft exceed our thought;
Lay all your wonted enmities aſleep,
From 'pards and tygers down to dogs and ſheep.
   Unanimous your Author bleſs,
   In all your diff'rent languages;
Whoſe providence preſerves each various beaſt,
All that in deſarts range, or paſtures reſt;
That company in herds, or ſingle ſtray,
And feeds the lion roaring for his prey.

XXXVII.
O ye Children of Man.

Man, ſum of beings! little world! where we
All nature in a point contracted ſee!
Where num'rous contradictions join in won-
   d'rous harmony!

                        Body

Body sustain'd by fleeting breath,
Immortal, liable to death.
Mind, that beyond the world can fly;
Yet chain'd to dust, must grov'ling lie;
Who all things seek to know with curious eye,
Yet to yourself, yourself a mystery.
When of th' amazing union you dispute,
Of thought with matter, and with angel brute.
Great monarch of all creatures here below,
Whate'er the Almighty pow'r and word did form;
Yet crush'd beneath the meanest, vilest foe,
Nearly allied to God, and kindred to the worm.
Bless God, who makes you over all things reign,
And after death reviv'd, a nobler kingdom gain;
Collective praises to your Sov'reign pay,
Who reigns alone supreme with everlasting sway.

XXXVIII.

O let Israel bless, &c.

Bless God, O Israel, his peculiar care,
For whom fix'd nature's rules inverted were;
    Divinely taught, divinely fed,
      With heav'nly laws, and angel's bread,
    And cloth'd by miracles, and led:
Egypt, sad theatre of judgment, sees
How vain t' oppress whom God to save decrees.
O'er burning sands the chosen fav'rites go,
Lo! from the stricken rock refreshing waters flow,
The travellers point out the river's course,
The river guides not here the travellers.

Jehovah't

Jehovah's self in person leads you on;
 Arms the creation for the war,
 The earth, the insects, and the air;
 Divides th' opposing seas, and stops the noonday sun;
For whom so many wonders wrought we see,
They loss almost their names by frequency.
Tune, tune your harps, and Sion's anthems sing,
To God your guide, your chief, your father, and your king.

XXXIX.
O ye Priests of the Lord, &c.

Bless God, ye priests, who at his altar wait,
 Chose from the chosen people of his love;
Who here your future bliss anticipate,
 And do on earth what angels do above.
Your hallow'd unction, heav'n's vicegerents share,
Should monarchs to usurp your honours dare.
Struck from above they die! for crimes alone;
Best typick mediators, you atone,
By death of beasts in feeble emblem shew
Sorer deaths to sinners due;
Ambassadors of peace, to God aspire,
Your breasts and altars touch with heav'nly fire;
 Before his footstool prostrate low,
 Yourselves as living victims show:
 Free from spot of worldly cares,
 Let your praise, and let your pray'rs,
As morning and as ev'ning incense rise,
Perpetual and accepted sacrifice.

XL. O

XL.

O ye Servants of the Lord, &c.

You that to his courts belong,
Sons of Levi, join the song:
In his temple, your abode;
Born the servants of your God.
To bear his ark with awful dread,
Round his altar daily tread;
And nightly banish dewy sleep,
Watches in his house to keep.
Safe arm'd with innocence you may despise,
  The threat'ning demagogue's and tyrant's frown;
The king that serves him not is slave to vice,
  The slave that serves him 'titled to a crown.
Ardent in praise of your great master be,
Whose service is alone true genuine liberty.

XLI.

O ye Spirits and Souls of the Righteous, &c.

Ye righteous souls from chains of body free,
Who long were tost on life's tempestuous sea,
Now landed safe in blest eternity.
For ever past this troublous fickle state,
Public distraction and domestic hate,
And wilful violence of the lawless great;
Who dar'd for right while here on earth be bold,
Nor cast by favour, nor weigh'd down by gold;
Nor longer taught by faith, by sight you know,
Justice is noblest wisdom here below;
Praise ye the judge, whose righteous doom will pay,
Just recompence to all at the great final day.

XLII.

O ye holy,

Bless God, ye saints, ye wise and happy few,
He his own image sees and loves in you;
Unmov'd by scoffers, who, with haughty air,
Dictate their follies from the scorner's chair.
 Where pleas'd and proud the idiots sit,
  Their pride the standard of their wit;
Frantic the shout, the jest, the mirth appears,
Which ends in fruitless and eternal tears.
Ye who from vice as from infection fly,
And care not to be damn'd for company:
Numbers to sin nor strength nor safety give,
'Tis better, tho' with few, to live,
Than die with many; in th' embattl'd field,
Who falls is dead as he that's singly kill'd.
Praise God, whose gracious pow'r has set you free
From guilt, the basest, heaviest slavery;
Praises to you peculiarly belong,
He, who your triumph gives, claims your triumphal song.

XLIII.

And humble Men of Heart, &c.

Ye humble men, who know all praise is due
To God supreme, and none to you;
Sole author of your good, and witness too;
Who fear applause, and greater pains bestow
In being pure, than seeming so.

Pride threw aspiring angels from the skies,
Humility their vacant thrones supplies,
And you, neglected here, low stooping thither rise.

 Th' eternal bless, who dwells on high,
 Who's ever to the lowly nigh;
Views from afar with scorn the sons of pride,
With humble contrite hearts delighted to reside.

XLIV.

O Hananiah, Azariah, and Mishael, bless, &c.

Let us, to sev'nfold fire condemn'd, in vain
Bless him whose nod can fiercest flames restrain;
God, the oppress'd all-gracious to defend,
God, of the friendless, never-failing friend;
Whoe'er vain idols to his throne would raise,
Against their aim yield matter for his praise;
If barb'rous demons human lives require,
Let sons of curs'd idolaters expire,
When pass'd to murd'rer Molech thro' the fire.

 Flames have idol gods subdued,
 Melted their ore, consum'd their wood;
 But seem discerning to revere
 Those who the God of Israel fear.
Thee, therefore, Lord, safe shielded by thy pow'r,
Thee, Son of God, Jehovah, we adore;
In form of man, descending to appear:
 To thee be ceaseless hallelujahs giv'n;
Praise, as in heav'n thy throne, we offer here;
 For where thy presence is display'd is heav'n.

The

The xix. Pfalm imitated.

THE wide extended empire of the skies,
Proclaims Jehovah's glory to our eyes;
The firmament above us where we stand,
Declares the work of his Almighty hand:
The ev'ning darkness, and the morning light,
Display his glory, wisdom, love, and might;
To ev'ry land their gen'ral voice extend,
Thro' all the world to earth's remotest end.
The morning sun arising from his place,
To shew thy glory, runs his daily race:
Thro' heav'n's high arches still he wings his way,
While fertile beams their genial heat convey.
His gracious law to souls with sin oppress'd,
Its precepts teach, its promise leads to rest:
And from his word such healing virtues rise,
As always tend to make the simple wise:
That heav'nly word affords us more delight
Than brightest gems when dazzling in our sight.
His sacred precepts still our footsteps guard;
In keeping them we find a great reward.
   His daily errors who can rightly find?
O! cleanse the latent faults of ev'ry mind.
My heart from all presumptuous vice restrain,
Nor over me let sin nor Satan reign.
Then shall my goings be establish'd right,
While pure and spotless in thy holy sight.
Whene'er I meditate upon thy ways,
Hear, aid, and still accept my feeble praise.

Divine Foreknowledge.

⁂ ETERNAL source of life, thou sov'reign King!
Thy pow'r I worship, and thy glory sing.
Before thy hands the starry heav'ns array'd;
Before this globe on fluid air was stay'd;
Before the variegated clouds on high,
Or rolling seasons e'er began to fly;
Ere pristine chaos into order ran,
Or yet thy Spirit had informed man,
Thy prescient knowledge ey'd with ample view
Thy various creatures, and their actions too;
The age, the station, birth, the time, the place,
Of all the children of the human race;
Our first rebellion 'gainst thy lawful sway,
With all its dire effects unto this day,
No change of state, nor empire e'er was heard,
But always to thy prescient eye appear'd.

A Morning Thought.

⁂ SEE how Aurora's blushing face appears,
While Phœbus from yon orient mountain rears;
The tow'ring larks around me gladly sing,
While with their sound the neighb'ring valleys ring;
The pearly drops of nightly dew decay,
Extinguish'd by the beams of rising day;
Th' expanding flow'rs their silken leaves unfold,
Rejoicing, now forget the ev'ning cold.
The active peasant hails the morning smile,
And by its beams forgets his weary toil.

The oxen low, the lambkins sportive play,
While shades of darkness flee the op'ning day.
Awake my soul! each creature round thee cries,
" Revere, adore, the Sov'reign of the skies!"

A Complaint.

*** ENVIRON'D by clouds of complicated grief,
Debar'd from hope, precluded from relief,
No mortal aid to mitigate my pain,
For help I cry, but still I cry in vain.
Thus burden'd, Lord, to thee for help I fly;
In this great conflict hear my bitter cry:
On thee I now my weighty burden cast,
Be thou my shadow from this stormy blast.
Let not my hope, my strength, nor courage fail,
When dangers threaten, let them not prevail:
Exert thy pow'r in this the evil day:
Stretch out thine arm, expel my griefs away:
Remove my sorrows, ease my burden'd mind;
For on thy mercy is my soul reclin'd.
If thou, O God! in love prolong'st my days,
They shall be spent in sounding forth thy praise:
And when at last I bid this life adieu,
In distant worlds the endless theme pursue.

On Israel's Passage from Egypt.

WHEN Egypt's king God's chosen tribes pursu'd,
In chrystal walls th' admiring waters stood.
When thro' the desert wild they took their way,
The rocks relented and pour'd forth a sea.

What

What limits can Almighty goodness know,
Since *seas* can harden, and since *rocks* can flow?

Divine Goodness.

⁎ THY boundless mercy still my life sus-
  tain'd,
When in the morning of my infant years,
Upon thy all-supporting arm I lean'd,
  Thro' ev'ry scene of life's perplexing cares.

II.

Thy mighty pow'r, the chariot of my soul,
  By which, when troops of danger took the
  field,
My soul secure did undejected roll,
  Upheld by thee, my safety and my shield.

III.

Thou art my hope, my confidence alone,
  My sure defence, my strength and only guide:
When ev'ry other spring of comfort's gone,
  Thy guardian mercies constantly abide.

IV.

To him whose tender and paternal care,
  Has led my soul thro' dark and rugged ways,
My grateful lips, enraptur'd shall prepare
  A song of thanks and everlasting praise.

A Call to Christian Activity.

⁎ AWAKE my soul, thy moments quick-
  ly fly,
Thy latest hour of mortal life is nigh;
This wilderness is not thy native clime;
Short and uncertain is thy point of time:

All'

All sublunary pleasures are but toys,
Compar'd with heav'n's never-fading joys.
There faith presents to thy observing eyes
An endless life of bliss that never dies.
What madness then in mortals to forego
This endless bliss, and court eternal woe!
Swift as thy fleeting transcient moments fly,
So swiftly run in virtue's placid way.
The most advantage we from vice can gain,
Are but short pleasures for eternal pain!

Happiness.

WHATEVER diff'rent paths mankind pursue,
 Oh, happiness! 'tis thee we keep in view!
'Tis thee in ev'ry action we intend,
The noblest motive and superior end!
Thou dost the scarcely finish'd soul incline;
Its first desire, and conscious thought, is thine;
Our infant breasts are sway'd by thee alone,
When pride and jealousy are yet unknown.
Thro' life's obscure and wild variety,
Our stedfast wishes never start from thee.
Thou art, of all our waking thoughts, the theme;
We court thee too in ev'ry nightly dream;
Th' immortal flame with equal ardour glows,
Nor one short moment's intermission knows;
Whether to courts or temples we repair,
With restless zeal we search thee ev'ry where:
Whether the roads that to perdition lead,
Or those which guides us to the stars we tread:
Thine is the hope, th' inestimable prize,
The glorious mark on which we fix our eyes!

Delusion

Delusion detected.

⁂ WHEN all the fleeting joys of time I view
As morning clouds, or as the early dew,
How soon they vanish, and how quickly fled,
With blasted hopes implanted in their stead.
Here *pride* laments her unregarded tone;
Expiring, breathes her last convulsive groan.
There death, regardless of the parent's cries,
In lasting slumbers seals the *infant's* eyes.
Attractive *beauties* likewise soon decline,
Impair'd by sickness or the wreck of time.
Tho' death a while th' impending blow suspends,
At last dismembers dear united *friends*.
The wretched *miser*, with his hoarded pence,
Deaf to the cries of want and indigence,
Ere long with grief must take his parting view,
And bid his dear, his only god adieu.
The daring *Hector*, and the modish *beau*,
In strength and dress that still unrivall'd go;
The one, at last, tho' insolent and proud,
Submits a victim to the reptile croud;
The outside paintings of the other fool,
Decay when tutor'd in affliction's school.
See how surrounding objects daily show
The fluctuating state of all below!

On the Phrase, "Killing Time."
Time is supposed to speak.

THERE's scarce a point wherein mankind agree
So well as in their boast of killing me;

I boast

I boast of nothing; but when I've a mind,
I think, I can be even with mankind.

An ardent Wish.

⁂ THOU source of life, this only blessing grant,
   At which my daily longing soul aspires,
A pious fervent heart from thee I want;
   This is the utmost height of my desires.

II.

A peaceful temper, gracious Lord, impart;
   Free from all strife and turbulence of mind;
Abhoring ev'ry false and guileful art,
   To which an abject servile heart's inclin'd;

III.

A humble heart serenely calm and mild,
   In which untainted virtue ever lies:
Peaceful and inoffensive as a child,
   Whose daily thoughts and views to thee arise.

IV.

A heart resign'd in ev'ry state to thee,
   Ready thy gracious pleasure to obey;
From ev'ry vice and ev'ry passion free,
   Submissive to thy universal sway.

A Significant Hint.

⁂ BEWARE to whom your *secrets* ye impart,
   Here always join your innocence with art;
To greater danger we our cause expose,
When to our neighbour we the whole disclose.
If ye reveal your *secret*—from that hour
It is not your's—but in another's pow'r;
And your example is a fair pretext
For confidents to *blab* it to the next!

Observe

Observe this *hint*, ye aged and ye young,
Know when to speak, and when to hold your tongue.
Epitaph.

GAILY I liv'd, as ease and nature taught,
And spent my little life without a thought:
And am amaz'd, how death, that tyrant grim,
Should *think* of me, who never *thought* of him!

On seeing the Sun rise.

*** LO! now the *sun's* refulgent beams arise
To banish darkness from the low'ring skies;
Thro' amber clouds behold his chariot driv'n,
In all the pomp and majesty of heav'n.
Night's sable curtains at *his* presence fly,
While limpid light hails ev'ry op'ning eye;
See how his gentle and transparent beams
Dart on the hills, and tremble on the streams:
At *his* approach the yielding moon retires,
And ev'ry star before *his* face expires.
To *him* the tow'ring lark expands her wings,
And with her morning notes the valley rings;
Each warbling songster hails his chearing ray,
While nature welcomes the approaching day;
The op'ning flow'r his genial virtue feels,
While all his orient lustre he reveals.
Altho' this sun with wonder I behold,
Shining in brightness like the sparkling gold,
Yet greater pomp I'll see, than Phœbus wears,
When the *bright Sun of Righteousness* appears.

Eternity.

CAN *Newton's* pupils tell ere time be past,
How many hours eternity will last?

Can he who scann'd the holy city * say,
When *sets* the sun of an eternal day?
Or can *Jehovah*, heav'n's omniscient King,
Say when his holy angels *cease* to sing?

A Midnight Meditation.

TO thee, all glorious, ever blessed pow'r,
  I consecrate this solemn silent hour,
While darkness robes in shades the spangled sky,
And all things hush'd in peaceful slumbers lie.
Unweary'd let me praise thy holy name;
Each thought with rising gratitude inflame,
For the rich mercy which thy hands impart,
Health to my limbs and comfort to my heart.
Should the scene change, and pain extort my sighs,
Then see my tears, and listen to my cries:
Then let my soul by some blest forecast know
Her sure deliv'rance from eternal woe.
Arm'd with so bright a hope, no more I'll fear
To view the dreadful hour of death draw near;
But my faith strength'ning as my life decays,
My dying breath shall mount to heav'n in praise;
O! may my pray'rs before thy throne arise,
An humble, but accepted sacrifice;
Bid kindly sleep my weary eye-lids close,
And cheer my body with a soft repose;
Their downy wings may guarding angels spread,
And from all dangers screen my helpless head;
May, of thy gracious light, some pow'rful beams
Shine on my soul, and sanctify my dreams.

* Rev. xxi. 15.

S *Pleasure.*

Pleasure.

PLEASURES are few, and fewer we enjoy:
And like quick silver, they are bright and coy.
We strive to grasp them with our utmost skill:
Oft they elude us, yet they glitter still.
If seiz'd at last, compute your mighty gains:
What are they, but rank poison in your veins?

On hearing a passing Bell.

THE solemn death *bell* tolls! a spirit's gone
To meet Jehovah on his awful throne:
Ye village-swains the solemn sound improve,
Make God your friend, and taste his boundless love.
While thoughtless numbers, void of heav'nly grace,
Forget their Maker, to their soul's disgrace.
Inspir'd by thee, *O bell!* my thoughts survey,
How fleeting life! how brittle human clay!
I, tho' a youth, strong death's resistless pow'r
May doom to fall before another hour.
O grant me, triune God! renewing grace,
Prepare, my soul, to meet thy Judge's face,
That I may join with all the blest above
To sing the greatness of redeeming love.

1 Sam. xxviii, 14. " *Saul perceived that it was Samuel.*"

NO wily fiend by magic spell,
Invok'd from his infernal cell,
To personate the prophet true,
But Samuel's self appears in view;

To make the prostrate king relent,
Humbly accept his punishment;
To warn him of his instant doom,
But not denounce the wrath to come.

Verse 19. "*To-morrow shall thou and thy Sons be with me.*"

WHAT do these solemn words portend?
    A gleam of hope when life shall end:
" Thou and thy sons, tho' slain, shall be
" To-morrow in repose with me!"
Not in a state of hellish pain,
If Saul with Samuel doth remain;
Not in a state of damn'd despair,
If loving Jonathan is there.

Words and Pronounciation.

IN all your words let energy be found,
    And learn to rise in sense and sink in sound;
Harsh words, tho' pertinent, uncouth appear,
None please the fancy that offend the ear.

The Criminal.—An Elegy.

*** AROUND my cell in active circles play
    The sons of freedom and of pleasure bland,
In jocund pastime spend the festive day,
    And taste the sweets of life on ev'ry hand.

II.

When Phœbus' purple beams adorn the west,
    And warblers rouse them with their matin song;
Each leaves his downy pillow's balmy rest,
    To re-assemble with the sportive throng.

III.

Abroad his friend the tedious hour beguiles,
   Delightful scenes regale his chearful soul;
At home the table, load with plenty, smiles,
   And care's forgotten o'er the flowing bowl.

IV.

Unpitied sorrows ne'er invade his peace,
   Distractive fears before his pleasure flee;
But hourly haunt this grief-fomenting place,
   Th' abode of darkness, wretchedness, and me.

V.

Once freedom o'er me wav'd her olive wand,
   Like you, elate I gladly hail'd the morn;
Was chief conductor of the sportive band;
   From them 'twas death to think of being torn.

VI.

Freedom, thou much abused bliss divine,
   How have I lavish'd all thy gifts away;
When circumscrib'd by thy impartial line,
   I spurn'd thy gentle and pacific sway.

VII.

Allur'd by folly's soft enchanting strain,
   I quite subdu'd my reason to its pow'r:
Abandon'd pleasure and illicit gain,
   Brought me, alas! to this untimely hour.

VIII.

Immur'd within this dismal vault I lie,
   Pity is deaf to my repeated calls;
I spend in vain my grief-extorted sigh,
   And breathe my sorrows to these gloomy walls.

IX. When

IX.

When Phœbus opes the morning gates of light,
    And mounts his golden car of state supreme;
To all but me, the heart-rejoicing sight
    Affords a chearful and reviving beam.

X.

When sable curtains round the world are spread,
    And Morpheus reigns o'er all the vast profound;
My groaning sighs, while others rest in bed,
    Excite the pity of the list'ning ground.

XI.

Whene'er th' unbolted massy gate expands,
    Which shuts me up within this vaulted room;
My shiv'ring mind with heart-struck panic stands
    In dread suspence to hear my instant doom.

XII.

When pity moves a philanthropic heart,
    To visit me within this lone retreat:
I wish, yet tremble lest he should impart
    The public's thought about my wretched fate.

XIII.

Imagination paints before my view
    The sad transactions of that fatal day;
When I, expos'd amid th' assembled crew,
    Infringed justice legal debt must pay.

XIV.

At times I think the evidences brought
    Against me, may not possibly agree
May not evince the crimination sought,
    And I thro' that obtain my liberty.

XV.

But soon, alas! these golden dreams subside,
  The pleasing phantom quickly disappears;
And rising sorrow, like a flowing tide,
  Extorts a stream of unaffected tears.

XVI.

Hither, ye unrestricted lawless throng,
  View me, sad emblem of your future state;
These unavailing tears of mine, ere long,
  Will, unrepenting, be your hapless fate?

An Elegy in Memory of the Rev. Mr G—d of C—d.

⁂ WHAT do these doleful plaintive notes portend,
  That rouse my slumbers and invade my ear?
Why does yon lofty turret mourning send
  A languid peal to swell the flowing tear?

II.

Why does each rural swain a-mourning go?
  Why heaves the sigh in ev'ry breast I see?
Why thus abandon'd to despairing woe?
  Why leave your joy to profligates and me?

III.

The sad reply, who can supinely hear,
  Let ev'ry tongue his early fate deplore;
Who can refuse to drop a languid tear,
  The friend of man and virtue is no more!

IV.

Behold his flock in concert sadly mourn,
  The starting tear appears in ev'ry eye;
While friends devout to his untimely urn
  The grateful tribute of an artless sigh.

V. O

V.

O death! terrific is thy mortal dart;
　Unseen thine arrows, unrepell'd thy pow'r,
And steel'd with rigour is thy flinty heart,
　In that important last decisive hour.

VI.

If pious virtue could avert thy blow,
　The faithful pastor, or the steady friend,
The streaming tear would not so early flow,
　Lamenting, G—d, thy much regretted end.

VII.

His scatter'd flock along the mountains roam,
　To ev'ry wolf and ev'ry snare a prey;
While he exulting is conducted home,
　To join the sacred legions of the sky.

VIII.

Break off your tears, suppress your mourning strain,
　When all your cares and all your toils are o'er,
Your faithful shepherd you shall meet again,
　Where death, and pain, and parting, are no more.

The First Psalm imitated.

*** HOW blest is he that never joins
　　With wicked men, to share
Their lawless pleasure; but declines
　　The swift deluding snare.

II.

Yet to the lone sequester'd grove,
　He frequently retires;
And ev'ry mandate from above
　He solemnly admires.

III. His

III.

His blossom, like the cedar tree,
    Unfading beauty beams;
Or like the verdant canopy,
    Impending o'er the streams.

IV.

But haughty sinners who despise
    The institutes of heav'n,
Like blasted leaves when winds arise,
    Shall be incessant driv'n.

V.

What tho' a while the godly man
    Is by affliction prest;
Yet vicious sinners never can
    Disturb his future rest.

VI.

The paths of those whom God approves
    Are open to his view;
But wrath and judgment from above,
    Shall wicked men pursue.

The Incomprehensibility, &c. of God.

BEYOND the utmost reach of reason's eye,
    Conceptions farthest stretch how far above!
Where bright imagination ne'er can fly,
    Tho' she excursive far and wide can rove.

In glory's bright effulgence, Pow'r Divine,
    Beaming perpetual rays of beauty bright,
Hath ever shone, and shall for ever shine
    In boundless wisdom, majesty, and might.

* *By G. K. Esq;*

Holy and pure, and in himself possest
  Of all perfection, passing all degree;
For ever blessing, and for ever blest!
  All happy those who all his glory see!
Whose boundless will gave time a bounded space,
  Whose word of pow'r unnumber'd systems rais'd;
Whose wisdom gave to each its proper place,
  From nothing calling ev'ry thing he pleas'd.
Who fills the whole, nor is by all contain'd,
  Unchangeable, tho' giving change to all!
Comprising all, whom none can comprehend,
  Who, when he wills, can time and change recall.
Of other spheres and systems all around,
  And their inhabitants while here below;
His ways, his works, his wisdom so profound,
  Our knowledge is to know we nothing know.
In this small planet's proper circle we
  By contemplation's pow'r his footsteps trace,
Admire how pow'rful great and good is he!
  Adore his wisdom, mercy, love, and grace.
On man alone, and none but man bestow'd,
  An emanation from his essence pure;
Superior reason from his bounty flow'd,
  In living souls for ever to endure.
Of those (by faded reason's darken'd light)
  Imagination wanders wide astray:
But all enliv'ning revelation bright,
  Hath shewn to endless life the living way!

When

When this immortal breath in man debas'd,
    And he by sin did forfeit ev'ry claim
To happiness, by justice unappeas'd,
    Consign'd to woe, to endless woe extreme.

To reconcile and for their guilt atone,
    By will divine, the filial Deity,
In whom all wisdom, grace, and mercy shone,
    Submitted innocent for them to die.

Because of his eternal essence they
    (To end with time incapable) partake;
His co-eternal love he did display,
    And sinless suffer'd for all sinners' sake.

So we, condemn'd by justice, rise by love,
    To mercy, grace, and happiness on high;
If we our faith and hope by virtue prove,
    From endless woe to joys that never die.

To him who gave, to him who so was giv'n,
    To him who brings this mercy, grace, and love
To three in one, and one in three in heav'n,
    Who lives and reigns supreme all worlds above:

To whom all kingdom, pow'r, and glory's due;
    Whose mercy, love, and grace to all extend;
Let all who live in adoration bow,
    And bless and praise him world without end!

Virtue.

WITH glitt'ring beams, and native glory bright,
Virtue nor darkness dreads, nor covets light;

But from her settled orb looks calmly down
On life or death, a prison or a crown.
Virtue's the' chiefest beauty of the mind,
The noblest ornament of human kind;
Virtue's our safe-guard, and our guiding star,
That stirs up reason when our senses err.
True sons of virtue mean repulse disdain,
Nor does their shining honour ever stain;
Their glorious minds are so securely great,
They neither swell nor sink at turns of fate.

Modesty.

IMMODEST words admit of no defence;
For want of decency is want of sense:
In modest actions there are certain rules,
Which to transgress confirms us knaves and fools.

An Epitaph on an Infant.

WHEN the archangel's trump shall blow,
    And souls to bodies join,
Millions shall wish their lives below,
    Had been as short as thine!

Charity, or Christian Love.

WHAT tho' I boast the ways of heav'n to scan,
In all the tongues and eloquence of man,
Or could I modulate with lips of fire,
In strains which list'ning angels might admire;
Did science her mysterious page unrol,
And with sublimer truths enlarge my soul;
Did prophecy, in one expanse of light,
Lay all the future open to my sight:

What

What tho' my faith all miracles display,
Bids plains ascend, and mountains melt away;
Rocks at my fiat into oceans hurl'd,
And earthquakes break the order of the world;
Or could I regulate th' obedient sun,
In other orbits bid the planets run,
Nature convuls'd, a different aspect wear,
Confound the seasons, and invert the year:
Yet did not charity its aid bestow,
Inspire my voice and in my bosom glow.
Tho' sweeter far than angels ever sung,
Persuasion on my lips enamour'd hung;
My fairest eloquence would scarce surpass
The tinkling cymbal or the sounding brass;
Faith, science, prophecy, would all expire,
Nor leave one spark to wake the dying fire.

 What tho' I consecrate my goods to bless,
And succour patient merit in distress,
Afflicted virtue of its tears beguile,
And bid the face of sorrow wear a smile;
Or could I, with the glorious three ally'd,
The fiery furnace unappal'd divide;
Yet did not charity possess my soul,
And all its pow'rs and faculties controul,
My most heroic fortitude were vain,
Patience of evil, and contempt of pain:
My gifts and alms the wretched to befriend,
In weakness would begin, in weakness end.

By

By my Friend the Rev. Mr J. T. when seemingly near death.

WITH admiration let me trace
    That hand of providence and grace,
        Which ev'ry want supplies;
Adore that pow'r which gave me birth,
And rais'd a clod of common earth
        To dwell above the skies.
'Tis just that he who gave me breath,
And still suspends the stroke of death,
        Should use me as he will;
Body and soul are in his hand,
My law shall be his mild command,
        Whether to spare or kill.
Great God! before thy throne I bow,
And if thine eyes behold me now
        The peaceful answer give:
Let thy own hand remove my pain,
And raise me to my strength again,
        And let thy servant live.
Not for myself nor worldly views,
Would I a larger portion chuse
        Of fleeting moments here;
But if it might a blessing prove
To those who share redeeming love,
        Thy cross I'll gladly bear.

Death.

CAN the deep statesman, skill'd in great design,
    Protract but for a day precarious breath?
Or the tun'd follower of the sacred nine,
    Soothe with his melody insatiate death?
        — *   T   No—

No—Tho' the palace bar her golden gate,
   Or monarchs plant ten thousand guards a-round;
Unerring and unseen, the shaft of fate
   Strikes the devoted victim to the ground;

What then avails ambition's wide stretch'd wing,
   The schoolman's page or pride of beauty's bloom!
The crape-clad hermit and the rich rob'd king,
   Levell'd lie mixt promiscuous in the tomb.

The Macedonian monarch wise and good,
   Bade, when the morning's rosy reign began,
Courtiers should call, as round his couch they stood,
   "Philip, remember thou'rt no more than man."

Search where ambition rag'd with rigour steel'd;
   Where slaughter like the rapid light'ning ran,
And say, while memory wipes the blood-stain'd field,
   Where lies the chief, or where the common man?

Vain are the pyramids and motto'd stones,
   And monumental trophies rais'd on high!
For time confounds them with the crumbling bones,
   That mix'd in hasty graves unnotic'd lie.

Rests not beneath the turf the peasant's head,
   Soft as the lord's beneath the labour'd tomb?
Or sleep's one colder in his close clay bed,
   Than t'other in the wide vault's dreary womb?
                            Hither

Hither let luxury lead her loose rob'd train
  Here flutter pride on purple painted wing;
And from the moral prospect, learn how vain
  The wish that sighs for sublunary things.

Ingratitude.

NO conduct can the human heart affect,
  So much as base returns or disrespect;
For when we've done as much as mortals can,
To serve the turn of an ungrateful man;
We're shock'd at wrongs that men may deign
    to give,
Tho' we regardless of God's bounties live:
But when ungrateful treatment moves my heart,
May it instruction to my mind impart:
While some with-hold their gratitude from me,
Be mine, all bounteous Father, paid to thee.

An Epitaph on Mrs * * *, *by her Husband.*

WHEN worth and truth like her's descend
    to dust,
Grief is a debt, and sorrow is most just;
Such cause had he to weep, who pious pays
This last sad tribute of his love and praise;
Who mourns the best of wives, and friends com-
    bin'd,
Where with affection diligence was join'd:
Mourns but not murmurs, sighs but not despairs;
Feels as a man, but as a Christian bears:
Trusts he shall meet her on that happy shore,
Where parting, pain, and death, shall be no more.

The following are taken from two pillars, which stood in the grove of a labyrinth, at a Nobleman's seat in Surry. On the top of each pillar is a human skull, said to belong to a former Lord and his Lady, who were the authors of the following lines, and who saw the pillars erected; and by their desires their skulls were placed there, at a certain number of years after their decease.

Lines on the Nobleman's Pillar.

WHY start? the case is your's, or will be soon,
Some years perhaps, perhaps another moon.
Life in its utmost span is still a breath,
And those who longest dream must wake at death:
Like you, I once thought ev'ry bliss secure;
And gold of ev'ry ill the certain cure.
Till steep'd with sorrow, and besieg'd with pain,
Too late I found all earthly riches vain.
Disease, with scorn, threw back the sordid fee,
And death still answer'd, what is gold to me?
Fame, titles, honours, next I vainly sought;
And fools obsequious, nurs'd the childish thought.
Gilded with brib'd applause, and purchas'd praise,
I built on endless grandeur, endless days;
But death awak'd me from a dream of pride,
And laid a prouder beggar by my side.
A loathsome carcase was my chiefest care,
And worlds were ransack'd but for me to share.
  Go on, vain man! in luxury be firm,
But know thou feasteth, but to feast a worm.

Already

Already sure less terrible I seem,
And you like me can on that letter dream;
Whether that dream may boast the longest date,
Farewell! remember, lest you wake too late.

Lines on the Lady's Pillar.

BLUSH not, ye fair, to own me, but be wise;
Nor turn from sad mortality your eyes.
Fame says, and fame alone can say how true,
I once was lovely, and belov'd like you.
Where are my vo'tries where my flatt'rers now?
Fled with the subject of each lover's vow.
Adieu! the rose is fled, the lily white;
Adieu, those eyes! that made the darkness light.
No more, alas! the coral lip is seen;
No longer breathe the fragrant gales between.
Turn from your mirror, and behold in me,
At once, what thousands cannot, dare not see.
Unvarnish'd, I, the real truth impart,
Nor here am plac'd, but to direct the heart;
Survey me well, ye fair ones, and believe
The grave may terrify, but can't deceive.
On beauty's frailties now no more depend,
Here youth and pleasure, age and sorrow, end:
Here drops the mask, here shuts the final scene,
Nor differs grave threescore from gay fifteen.
All pleas'd alike to that same goal, the tomb,
Where wrinkled Laura smiles at Chloe's bloom.
When coxcombs flatter, and when fools adore,
Learn hence the lesson to be vain no more.
Yet virtue still against decay can arm,
And even lend mortality a charm.

Captain ———'s Excuse for not fighting a Duel.

WHAT! you're afraid then? Yes, I am;
    you're right:
I am afraid to sin, but not to fight.
My country claims my service; but no law
Bids me in folly's cause my sword to draw;
I fear not man, nor devil; but, tho' odd,
I'm not asham'd to own, I fear my God!

An Elegy. Written in a Garden.

WHAT mingled beauties here conspire to
    please?
What various prospects cheer the wand'ring eye!
In these sweet shades let me recline at ease,
    While balmy Zephyrs fan the sultry sky.

Here polish'd art assumes fair nature's face:
    Round the smooth bush the woodbines breath
        perfumes!
Here tufted pinks the mossy margin grace,
    And the sweet rose in sov'reign beauty blooms.

Elate with spring, and dress'd in all her dyes,
    See hov'ring round—Yon insect idly gay;
A moment on its balmy breast she lies,
    Then light thro' liquid ether wings her way.

Thou beauteous trifler, can so fine a form
    Sustain black boreas, and benuming frost?
Or when black skies discharge th' impetuous
    storm,
    Must all thy transient elegance be lost.

Go where the gay Belinad reigns confest,
  Despotic sov'reign of the youthful train;
While her bright eyes explore thy varied vest,
  Thy little life shall moralize my strain.

While to her sight thy gaudy wings are spread,
  If the light show'r, or gentlest dew descend,
Thy momentary age of mirth is fled;
  And the gay dreams of golden summers end.

In thee, perchance, the thoughtless Nymph may view
  The changeful emblem of her blooming face;
As soon disease may that fair form subdue,
  And each external excellence debase.

Then will th' admiring crowd no longer lend;
  No more sweet adulation soothe her ear;
No more th' assidous youth her steps attend;
  No more her smiles on ev'ry face appear.

Divine Love.

WHAT is more tender than a mother's love,
  To the sweet infant fondling in her arms?
What arguments need her compassion move,
  To hear its cries, and help it in its harms?
Now if the tend'rest mother was possest
Of all the love, within her single breast,
Of all the mothers since the world began,
'Tis nothing to the love of God to man!

An Ode.

NO glory I covet, no riches I want;
  Ambition is nothing to me;
The one thing I beg of kind heav'n to grant
  Is a mind independent and free.

With

With passion unruffled, untainted with pride,
  By reason my life let me square;
The wants of my nature are cheaply supply'd,
  And the rest is but folly and care.

The blessings which providence freely has lent,
  I'll justly and gratefully prize,
While sweet meditation and cheerful content,
  Shall make me both healthy and wise.

How vainly thro' infinite trouble and strife,
  The many their labours employ!
Since all that is truly delightful in life,
  Is what all, if they will, may enjoy.

Riches.

WHAT man in his wits, had not rather be poor,
  Than for lucre his freedom to give?
Ever busy the means of his life to secure,
  And so ever neglecting to live.

Environ'd from morning to night in a cloud,
  Not a moment unbent or alone:
Constrain'd to be abject, tho' ever so proud,
  And at ev'ry one's call but his own.

Still repining and longing for quiet each hour,
  Yet studiously flying it still;
With the means of enjoying his wish in his pow'r,
  But accurs'd with his wanting the will.

For a year must be past, or day must be come,
  Before he has leisure to rest:
He must add to his store this or that pretty sum,
  And then will have time to be blest.

But

But his gains more bewitching the more they
 increase,
 Only swell the desire of his eye :
Such a wretch let mine enemy live if he please,
 Let not even mine enemy die.

Against Life.

WHAT path of *life* by man is trod,
 Without *repenting* of the rod?
Business is tumult, noise, and jar;
At *home* is weariness and care:
The *ocean* storm and terror yields;
And painful toil and sweat the *fields:*
Abroad you're destitute, if *poor*;
If *rich*, endanger'd by your store;
By griefs the *nuptial state* is torn;
The *single* friendless and forlorn.
With *children* sorrows still increase;
Childless, we moan our barrenness.
Folly our giddy *youth* insnares;
And weakness sinks our *hoary hairs.*
The wise this only choice *would* try,
Or not to live, or soon to die.

For Life.

WHAT path of *life* by man is trod,
 Without *rejoicing* at the rod?
From *business*, wealth and wisdom flows;
At *home* is pleasure and repose.
The *ocean* gainful traffic yields,
And nature cheers us in the *fields.*

Abroad

Abroad you're less expos'd, if *poor*;
If *rich*, respected for your store.
More bliss the *nuptial state* receives,
The *single* more in freedom lives.
The *parent's heart* with transport swells,
And less of care the *childless* feels:
Our *youth* firm health and vigour shares:
And rev'rence crowns our *hoary hairs*.
The wise this choice would *never* try,
Or not to live, or soon to die.

Epitaph.

A PLEASING form, a firm, yet cautious mind,
Sincere, tho' prudent; constant, yet resign'd;
Honour unchang'd, a principle profest,
Fix'd to one side, but moderate to the rest:
An honest courtier, and a patriot too;
Just to his prince, and to his country true;
Fill'd with the sense of age, the fire of youth;
A scorn of wrangling, yet a zeal for truth;
A generous faith, from superstition free;
A love to peace, and hate of tyranny;
Such this man was, whom now from earth remov'd,
At length enjoys the liberty he lov'd.

Mutual Forbearance recommended.

*⁎*SEE how the various sects discord;
Like hostile bands appear;
And men, who serve one common Lord,
Each other bite and tear.

The vot'ries of the papal chair,
    Cry hell shall be the doom
Of ev'ry tribe who dare appear
    Without the Church of Rome.
And some who think religion lies
    In party-zeal and strife,
Roundly assert, a Roman dies,
    Cut off from endless life.
Ye breathing clods of mortal clay,
    Who damn whoe'er ye please;
Can you disclose in open day
    Your Maker's dark decrees?
Many, I hope, that you abhor,
    Are now with God in heav'n;
And *some, I fear,* whom ye adore,
    Are from his presence driv'n.
Suspend your rage from those without,
    Your greatest foe's within,
Your chiefest enemies, I doubt,
    Are *Satan, self,* and *sin.*

The Power and Goodness of God.

*** DREAD sov'reign, how amazing are thy ways,
Surpassing all our knowledge and our praise,
Thy *pow'r* the wide extended heav'ns rear'd.
At thy command the sun and moon appear'd:
By thee the wheels of time do daily run,
While heav'nly roads are measur'd by the sun:
The foaming brine confess thy mighty sway,
And wind and storms their Maker's voice obey:
                              By

By thee, the lofty pines expand and grow,
And bending, praise thee in each fruitful bough:
The num'rous flocks that haunt the downy meads,
Thy *pow'r* created, and thy *goodness* feeds.
To thee, the plumy warblers of the spring,
In grateful accents mount the air and sing:
To man thy pow'r and goodness still appear,
In ev'ry season of the rolling year:
While storms in winter clarify the air,
And for the seed the fruitful fields prepare;
The liquid drops their genial virtue bring,
And gladly hasten to salute the spring:
The beams of summer bring so sweet a smile,
That autumn's blessings recompence our toil.
Thus, by rotation, seasons as they roll,
Thy pow'r and *goodness* constantly extoll?

Creation.

*** WHEN darkness held on unmolested sway,
And night was undistingush'd from the day;
'Twas then, the mighty Sov'reign of the skies
Bad light and order from confusion rise:
The system by his wisdom was devis'd,
While on the air, this earthly ball he pois'd,
And as a tent with curtains fine array'd,
Above our heads the heav'ns he display'd:
At his command the earth and seas divide,
Each to their station stedfastly abide:
He gave the warbling tenants of the sky
A tuneful voice, with golden wings to fly;

He

He form'd the herds, and still preserves their brood
By verdant pasture for their daily food:
His hand adjusted ev'ry rolling sphere,
And bade the shining orbs of light appear:
And to conclude the preconcerted plan,
He form'd his highly favour'd creature, man:
And man, with lordly pow'r he did invest,
In wisdom far superior to the rest:
These *few* are works of his Almighty hand,
'Tis but a *few* that we can understand.

An Elegy to the Memory of Mrs Garden of Delgaty.

⁂ WHILE the full breast heaves with a plaintive sigh,
While artless tears flow from the languid eye,
While tender strains of unaffected woe,
By nature taught from ev'ry bosom flow,
I, at her tomb, an obscure friend appear,
To drop a grateful, tho' a fruitless tear;
This little tribute to her dust I pay,
And call her virtues into open day.
   Bless'd with each grace that possibly could please;
With youth, with beauty, elegance, and ease:
Her fertile mind with useful knowledge fraught,
Improv'd by learning, and refin'd by thought:
How frequently her tender heart arose,
At painted tales of visionary woes!
Whene'er the orphan or the widow cry'd,
Their pinching want her ready hand supply'd:

Behold the num'rous sons of want, and see
Them mingling tears of gratitude with me!
Virtue and wealth, (which seldom are conjoin'd)
To raise her merit, mutually combin'd:
Loving and tender in relation's ties,
Ready to aid, and prudent to advise:
Witness the hour unfeeling death drew nigh,
And rob'd her of her bliss * beneath the sky.
O fatal *hour!* let memory still report;
Her stay behind how transient, and how short!
While her dear consort, and her bosom friend,
Slow pac'd, approached to his latter end;
Resolv'd his trouble and his pain to share,
Lo, at his side, her unremitting care
Still watch'd with love, hope, fear, and sleepless
 eyes!
Bathed in tears, and swell'd by throbbing sighs,
How thin'd the nurse, the lover, and the wife,
'Till the last hour of his expiring life?

 If such endowments in a human heart,
Could death's too early falling stroke avert,
My languid muse would not have cause to mourn,
So prematurely o'er her silent urn.

 Life, what art thou in all thy blooming height?
A flow'r, a cloud, a phantom, in our sight!
Thy blandishments no sooner felt than gone,
Cropt like some blossom ere 'tis fully blown:
Or as some meteor, thro' the shades of night,
Displays a transient, momentary light;

 * Her Husband.

A

A limpid flame, whose bright effulgent ray,
Kindles and blazes, breaks and dies away.
Just emblem this, of all the human race!
How soon we hasten to one common place!
Where she is gone, for whom is taught to flow,
Th' unbidden tear of sympathizing woe.

When heav'n's high mandate bade her virtue try,
That last great bus'ness of mankind, to die!
Prepar'd, resign'd, she with a pleasing smile,
Welcomes the hour that ends her worldly toil.

She's gone! Who shall her orphans loss repair?
What friend shall tend them with a mother's care?
Who shall inspire their minds with virtuous truth?
Or guard their lives against the snares of youth?
O early fled from their belov'd embrace!
In whom was center'd all her happiness,
Far distant fled into the silent tomb,
And lost untimely in her vernal bloom.

Yet why regret her exit with such pain!
Our temp'ral loss is her eternal gain:
Why mourn her loss?—when fled to heav'nly joys,
Far from a world of tumult, care, and noise.
Nor pain, nor passion, rage, nor envy's there,
The frowns of fortune, nor the stings of care:
There no distraction marrs her pleasing song,
Surrounded by the blest angelic throng:

There, from the source of life, a cheering ray,
Of beams divine, shine thro' eternal day!

On being asked, What is the greatest Blessing on Earth?

PEACE, health, and strength, food, raiment, and content;
A heart well manag'd, and a life well spent;
A soul devoted, and a thirst for God;
Courting his smile, but patient of his rod;
Each day more fit to breathe its latest breath,
And then the most alive when nearest death.

The Widow's Son of Nain paraphrased *.

*** IN Palastine, near Jordan's flow'ry plain,
A matron dwelt, a villager of Nain:
Who long had trode on life's uncertain stage,
Deprest with sorrows and declining age.
Her dearest friend, her guardian, and her guide,
Insatiate death had taken from her side:
The faithful matron, much dejected, gave
His dear remains with sorrow to the grave;
And paid the tribute of unfeigned tears,
Till time had measur'd nearly twenty years;
For many a season did revolving turn
Before this widow had forgot to mourn.

The father's death a blooming youth surviv'd,
And both at strength and manhood soon arriv'd:
The tender matron felt a rising joy
Inspire her breast while she beheld the boy;
At once an emblem to remind his mother
Of both her husband, father, and her brother.

* See Luke vii. 11.

'Tis

'Tis he alone abates her flowing tears,
Her chief supporter thro' declining years.
To the Almighty ruler of the skies,
In his behalf her pray'rs incessant rise;
And ev'ry day implores the boon from heav'n,
That grace and virtue to the youth be giv'n.
Was full resign'd to all that God had done,
He took the father, but he spar'd the son.
The blooming youth, his mother's only care,
For both their wants did ardently prepare.
Her former grief did artfully beguile,
And caus'd her face resume a chearful smile:
The matron finds her sorrows calmly rest,
And of her son and happiness possest.

But ah! how transient ev'ry scene below!
How short our bliss! how permanent our woe!
While brooding hope expands her tow'ring
    wings,
To taste the cup that future comfort brings;
A feeble touch retards our fancied gain,
And renders all our future prospects vain:
So bright a landscape nature never drew,
As fruitful fancy paints before the view.

Our widow's son with all her hopes decay;
For pining sickness wastes him ev'ry day:
Physicians try'd each human art in vain,
To cure the patient, or abate his pain;
Yet unavailing was their skilful art,
To turn aside the swift-descending dart:
He fell a victim to that mortal foe,
Who sweeps from earth his thousands at a blow.

To poignant grief the matron now is driv'n,
Entirely wrench'd of ev'ry stay, but heav'n.
No filial hand to wipe away her tears;
No darling son to soothe a mother's cares.
Her child, her husband, and her pleasure gone;
And left a prey to wretchedness alone.
   Around her now the citizens repair,
Condole the loss of her apparent heir;
With her again they tread the rueful way,
To leave the son's beside the father's clay.
But lo! what mercies quickly interpose,
To raise their wonder and abate their woes;
The *Great Physician* sent from God appears,
T' assuage her grief, and wipe away her tears:
He view'd the bier, beheld the mourning train,
And felt compassion beat thro' ev'ry vein.
Requests the mother to suspend her woe,
Till he his pow'r and loving-kindness show:
And then, with glowing ardour in his eyes,
Address'd the corse, and said "Young man,
      ARISE!"
The great behest awakes the silent dead,
The youth revives, and lifts his drooping head:
The breathless clay his spirit reinforms;
The Lord consigns him to his mother's arms:
While she, enraptur'd with extatic joy,
Once more embrac'd her dear and only boy.
Uplifted hands and voice she rear'd to heav'n,
And bless'd Immanuel for the treasure giv'n:
Confess'd him God the Saviour, full of grace,
The Judge, the Maker of the human race.
                      On

On all the scene her wond'ring neighbours gaz'd,
Th' eternal Father's pow'r and goodness prais'd;
Ador'd the mighty Potentate of heav'n,
Who had to man such gracious favours giv'n.
   Now smiling joy in ev'ry face appears,
The nearest friends forget their weeping tears:
The widow's son, (the chearful strain went round,)
Was dead, but lives; was lost, but now is found.
The aged matron spent her future days
In acts of virtue, piety, and praise:
And 'till her faithful course on earth was run,
Was kindly nourish'd by her only son.

TIME: PART OF AN ELEGY,
Written near the Ruins of Elgin Cathedral.
PART II.

TO mark th' unwearied flight of rolling years,
   The vanities of life, the wastes of time;
To point man's happiest hopes, t' alarm his fears;
   The muse again awakes the moral rhyme.
She marks those states alternate rise and fall,
   That once o'er all the imperial sceptre bore:
She marks those heroes drop that shook the ball,
   Whom fame, and flaming victory, flew before.
What cannot time destroy? those dazzling thrones
   Of Syria, Persia, or of Egypt old,
Where are they now? They rest with kingly bones,
   In the same moulder'd dust with heroes roll'd.
                                     Lo,

Lo, where PHILANDER's recent afhes fleep,
  The Loves and Graces in fad concert mourn!
Behold the friend, the parent, fifter, weep!
  And bathe, with many a tear the untimely urn.

But not their tears, nor all the wiles of art,
  Can ope the iron chambers of the tomb:
Not virtue's felf can move death's flinty heart,
  Nor youth, nor age, nor beauty's angel-bloom.

Behold what crowding graves! What emblems round!
  What living lectures breathe from ev'ry ftone!
No airy boaft of grandeur marks the ground;
  Thefe humble teachers talk of death alone.

" Come ye (they cry) in fortune's trappings dreft,
  " Ye fick for pow'r, ye fticklers for a name:
" Behold where you muft take your endlefs reft,
  " A bed of earth is all that ye can claim."

Perhaps fome fcutcheon, or fome ftately buft,
  Some fculptur'd urn with marble ftrong up-ftay'd,
May crown your grave,—yet thefe fhall fall to duft,
  And crumbling, mingle with the bones they fhade.

Behold thefe graves! the Young, the Vain, the Gay!
  How filent all! their fports now put to flight!
No voice of mirth is heard! no chearful play
  Awakes the flumber of eternal night.

Beneath

Beneath that mofs-grown ftone now mould'ring lie
   Thofe heav'nly charms that bade the world adore
The faultlefs fhape, foft air and fparkling eye,
   Were *Celia's* once, but *Celia's* now no more!
Yet thus fhall fade the faireft charms below,
   Of art or nature, body or of foul:
Like northern lights, or like the painted bow,
   So fwift of human life the meteors roll.

PART III.

SHALL then thefe eyes no more the fun behold?
   Muft I too fleep in Death's all-darkfome fhade?
" His mortal race is run," the tale be told,
   " Low lies his head on yonder dufty bed."
So when the deftin'd years their courfe have run,
   And mortals tread the path they trod before;
My name or birth-place fhall no more be known,
   Eraz'd, like figures on the fandy fhore.
Yet why complain our fhort fpun lives expire,
   When nature fades, and ftars their darknefs mourn;
Since all alike partake th' Eternal fire,
   And all alike muft languifh in their turn?
The earth hath bloom'd; the clouds dropt fatnefs down;
   The felf-fame fun hath fhone with annual ray,
And rivers feen eternal, as they run,
   One generation rife, and one decay.

Yet all must fade, and suns grow dim with years,
　　Till brighter suns, and purer ether shine;
Till, at the last shrill trump, that morn appears,
　　When Heav'n's Eternal Day, O Man, is thine.

Meanwhile full seventy years are given to taste
　　Life's pleasing joys, or graver duties bear;
Then sated, tir'd,—we take our needful rest,
　　And yield to others all terrestrial care.

Let others build, or plant, or plough the deep,
　　More wealth atchieve, or better string the lyre;
Oft like ourselves at disappointment weep;
　　And weary, like ourselves, at last expire.

Alas, like magic, life's gay scenes decoy;
　　Of banquets rich we dream, and damsels fair;
Of gorgeous halls, and airs of heav'nly joy;
　　Then wake to disappointment and despair.

Even while the visionary glories shine,
　　And Fancy smiles to find them in her eye,
Lo Death! the dread magician, gives the sign,
　　And all the airy charms for ever fly.

PART IV.

HOW frail our bliss on Life's uncertain coast!
　　How vain our trust in all beneath the pole!
From care to care with fruitless anguish tost,
　　Till to th' eternal boundless sea we roll.

What more than madness thus to sport with fate,
　　To hang our fortunes o'er the rocky steep,
When the least breath of air may end their date,
　　And whelm for ever in the roaring deep!

　　　　　　　　　　　　　　　But

But hark! what sound invades my startled ear,
  Slow-pealing from yon turret's stately height!
—Again it tolls! resound Death's caverns drear,
  And distant echos fill the silent night.
Methinks, to Reason's sober ear it calls,
  " Be wise, and snatch the swift-departing hour;"
It bids gay *Florio* quit the midnight-balls,
  And court fair wisdom in her sacred bow'r.
It bids *Avarus* quit his earthly schemes,
  His houses, lands, and all his world of gain:
" Awake ambition, from thy golden dreams,
" Nor treasure to thyself a world of pain."
It warns us now; ere long shall warn no more,
  Till the last knell proclaim our endless doom:
Then ev'ry trial, ev'ry hope, is o'er;
  We take our long, long mansion in the tomb.
Methinks I hear the awful silent Dead,
  Echo assent thro' all their murm'ring cells:
Them Darkness covers with eternal shade,
  While smiling Hope in mortal mansions dwells.
—See the Sun labour in his course for man,
  The Air breathe balm, the Earth her bounty pour!
Year waits on year, to see him change his plan,
  But finds him idling on a barren shore.
Vain man! already half thy years are past:
  Life's little morning gone, the noon comes on;
It come, the ev'ning hastens on us fast,
  But ah, how little of thy work is done!
—Say,

—Say, why did Heav'n such active pow'rs
    bestow,
  Progressive still, and boundless in their aim?
Was it to grasp the paltry things below,
  And waste in vain their never-dying flame?
Was it to barter peace for golden ore;
  To toil; and count the rich the only Great?
Or still more wretched, sigh for pomp and pow'r,
  And all the weary pageantry of state?
Was it to pass in thoughtless joy the morn,
  To dress, to bow, to speak and smile with art,
Then flaunt abroad, thro' whirling pleasures
    borne,
  Nor steal one secret hour to mend the heart?
How sweet the joys that to the Good belong!
  (While Vice to Mis'ry leads, remorse or pain);
Collected, cool—far from the giddy throng,
  Those walk with Virtue, and ensure their gain.
Oft too, at rising morn, or setting day,
  They woo from heav'n Devotion's holy fire;
Around them angels wait in bright array,
  Smooth all their steps, and all their thoughts
    inspire.
Let Fortune rage, yet 'mid the storm, serene
  They smile: their stedfast anchor fix'd on high;
They see th' Eternal rule life's troublous scene,
  And trust their safety to a Father's eye.
Let Death approach, still leaning on their God,
  I see them firm that last sad combat brave;
See Death, their friend, to life direct the road,
  And dipt in balm his shafts, but wound—to save.
                        —But

—But stop, O Muse: now time to quit these
    iles:
Delight not all the bier, or solemn bell:
Thy serious strain the Gay may treat with smiles,
    Or say they lik'd a sprightlier full as well.

On the Death of a beautiful young Lady.

Attend to this important truth,
Ye gay of tender years;
On whom the rosy dawn of youth
In all its bloom appears.

CLARINDA just had number'd twenty
    springs,
Possess'd of all the charms that beauty brings;
Nature and art with ev'ry grace refin'd,
Conspir'd to form *Clarinda's* youthful mind,
While blooming health beat high in ev'ry vein,
And swains around her form'd a num'rous train;
Th' obsequious croud admir'd her angel form,
Endow'd with ev'ry captivating charm.
Large draughts of bliss her fruitful fancy drew,
And scenes of grandeur painted to her view:
Elate with joy, and big with promis'd gain,
Applauded hourly by th' admiring train.

But see how heav'n retards the rapid flight
Of human reck'ning daily in our sight;
Indignant, frust'rates all our airy dreams,
And marrs at once our best concerted schemes:
It crops our soaring plumes on ev'ry side;
Then smiling, mocks to see our falling pride.

'O transient joy! 'tis but a recent while
Since she dealt *heav'nly blessings* in her smile;
While *racks* and *tortures* in her frown appear'd,
The one was courted, and the other fear'd.
But now, alas! behold the blooming fair,
Defenceless, sickens at the breeze of air
That locks transpiring exhalations in,
While wand'ring pains and scorching heat begin:
Oppress'd with sickness, now *Clarinda* lies,
Languid her cheeks, and dim her sparkling eyes:
' The lovely nymph, dejected, hangs her head,'
Her lillies droop, and all her roses fade.
Now drugs and healing arts with speed appear,
While parents bathe her couch with many a tear;
But healing arts and parents mourning strain,
And groans, and clouds of rising sighs, are vain:
Increasing sickness, at the dire command,
Consigns her o'er to death's unfriendly hand.

    Ye belles, draw near, this fallen maid review,
No more the object of your envy now!
Where is the dazzling splendour of her eyes,
That struck each gazing stranger with surprize?
See where the lovely graces made their seat;
But cruel death impells their swift retreat:
Those rudy lips that once engag'd the fight,
Now pale as ashes form a ghastly white.

    Come now, ye lovers, view this pallid clay!
This transient, fleeting beauty of a day!
Will still your ardent love for her increase?
What fondest youth will flee to her embrace?

The lifeless corse with pleasing joy attend,
The blasted beauty of her face commend.

   Thus morning flow'rs display their fragrance sweet,
Nor dread the ev'ning cold, nor scorching heat:
But ere the sun has reach'd meridian noon,
The lovely blossom's wither'd and cut down.

   O ye, on whom youth's vernal bloom appears!
Improve with care your swift departing years;
And from *Clarinda's* exit learn to prize
The paths which lead to *life* that never dies.

MORAL EPIGRAMS.

On Friendship.

⁎ IN your researches if you chance to find,
    An honest faithful neighbour to your mind;
Who friendly paints without reserved guise,
Your vice and virtue clear before your eyes;
You well may boast of such intrinsic gain,
As *kings* or *princes* never can obtain!

On Oeconomy.

⁎ IN ev'ry sphere of life the centre chuse,
    Be neither meanly sordid nor profuse:
Should fortune o'er you spread her golden wings,
Nor hoard nor lavish what she kindly brings.
'Gainst future events providently save,
You know not what's between you and the grave:
I'd sooner far bequeath my greatest foe,
Than live dependent on a friend below.

On Vain Glory.

₀ HOW meanly rude is he who daily vaunts,
Of talents which he thinks his neighbour wants:
Tho' wanting yours, perhaps his honest mind
Possesses twenty of a better kind.

On Modern Friendship.

₀ WHEN instantaneous friendship is profest,
Then time and patience are the surest test,
To prove the man who lays a rapid claim
To faithful friendship's just endearing name.
The double-minded from a heart sincere,
In actions better than from words appear;
So ev'ry man (perhaps you'll think it odd)
Should use his friend as Moses did his rod:
While it retain'd its proper ancient form,
The prophet us'd it to support his arm:
But when his staff assum'd another hue,
The cautious Hebrew from the serpent flew *!

Thoughts on a Watch.

₀ THIS faithful menial serves me always right,
And duly points the hours both day and night.
O could my temper move like this machine,
'Nor urg'd by passion, nor delay'd by spleen.'
Like her be duly pois'd on ev'ry side,
Too high for meanness, and too low for pride.
Passive to virtue's regulating pow'r,
Nor idly waste thro' life a single hour:
A just memento daily learn from thee,
To serve my Maker as thou servest me.

* See Exod. iv. 3.

INDEX.

INDEX TO THE HYMNS.

A

	Page	Hymn
ALMIGHTY Sovereign of the skies	28	33
Almighty God, we now appear	48	61
An awful thought I call to mind	85	107
An outcast from my native clime	90	113
Alas! and did my Saviour bleed	100	126
Amidst my death-deserving sins	ib	127
A house remains not made with hands	102	129
Amazing grace to man appears	113	143
Again, indulgent Lord, I come	ib	144
Adore th' amazing pow'r of God	124	159
Arise, my soul, and quickly fly	126	163
Attend to this important truth	131	170
A charge to keep I have	132	171
An Angel from the rending sky	133	172
Almighty Ruler of the sky	138	178

B

By nature vile, conceiv'd in sin	17	13
Behold the Saviour of mankind	18	15
Behold him triumph o'er the grave	30	35
Behold what countless numbers stand	50	63
Before Jehovah's awful throne	54	68
Before the throne our Surety stands	56	71
Beneath a load of cares and years	61	78
By faith erect before your eyes	88	111
Before the starry frame was rear'd	97	123
Beware, my soul, of Satan's train	98	124
Beneath thy highly injur'd throne	101	128
Behold your dear Redeemer stands	127	164

	Page	Hymn
C		
Come let us join our chearful songs	12	5
Come, Father, Son, and Holy Ghost	44	54
Come, quickly come, most gracious Lord	47	59
Christ from the dead is rais'd and made	65	84
Come thou long expected Jesus	67	86
Come let us use the grace divine	106	134
D		
Did not thy wisdom from above	12	6
Despair and darkness fill my heart	25	28
E		
Eternal source of love divine	14	8
Eternal wisdom, we thee praise	74	96
Eternal beam of light divine	103	130
F		
Father, I stretch my hands to thee	13	7
Father, behold with gracious eyes	25	27
Father of Jesus Christ, my Lord	26	29
Forth in the morning, Lord, I go	42	52
Father, to thee we lift our eyes	44	55
From him who fills unbounded space	119	151
Father, thy mercy we implore	130	163
Father, how wide thy glory shines	131	169
G		
Great God, who from my early youth	22	23
Great Parent of the human race	45	57
Great God, at whose supreme command	80	101
Gentle and peaceful as a dove	106	135
Great God, with wonder and with praise	125	162
God of my life, whose gracious pow'r	138	177
H		
How blest is that angelic band	18	14
Hosanna to the Prince of light	19	17
How can a guilty sinner shun	24	26
How soon the blooming flow'rs decay	29	34
Holy as thee, O Lord! is none	73	94
Hail! Father, Son, and Holy Ghost	82	104
Hark how the Gospel trumpets sound	87	110
Hosanna with a chearful sound	95	120

	Page	Hymn
He dies, the friend of sinners dies	110	139
How patient is Almighty God	114	145
Hail boundless love that first began	115	146

I

	Page	Hymn
Jesus, an int'rest in thy blood	20	18
Justly incensed, holy Lord	21	20
In boundless mercy, gracious Lord, appear	22	21
Jesus, by thy redeeming blood	32	38
Jesus, Redeemer of mankind	33	39
Jesus, thy glory we confess	ib	40
Inspirer of the ancient seers	39	48
Jehovah sends a herald forth	65	83
In riches never make thy boast	67	87
Jesus, thou all-redeeming Lord	68	88
In fruitless toil the sons of men	69	89
I will not fear while Christ is near	70	91
In ev'ry hour, O God, thy pow'r	76	97
I feel the healthy springs of life	79	100
Jesus in our behalf has died	83	105
Jesus, may thy true members shine	89	112
In hope of joys to us unknown	94	119
Jesus, our great Redeemer's gone	96	121
In the dark regions of the deep	97	122
I want a principle within	118	150
Jesus, the friend of sinners, see	122	157
In boundless mercy Lord forgive	125	161
I long my Redeemer to see	129	167

L

	Page	Hymn
Lo! the young tribes of Adam rise	11	3
Lord, when I count thy mercies o'er	16	11
Lord, we admire thy mighty sway	16	12
Let all that breathe the vital air	26	30
Let ev'ry saint and ev'ry friend	27	31
Lord, where shall guilty souls retire	31	37
Let ev'ry tongue thy goodness speak	35	43
Lord, let my evening sacrifice	39	47
Lo! he comes with clouds descending	51	64
Lovers of pleasure more than God	70	90

Life

	Page	Hymn
Life like an empty vapour flies	121	154
Let heaven, and earth, and seas combine	134	174

M

	Page	Hymn
My God, my King, thy various praise	9	1
My grateful soul to thee, O Lord	10	2
My fainting soul, to thee, O God	11	4
My God, for all I am and have	41	50
Master supreme, to thee I cry	43	53
My God, to thee I lift my eyes	58	74
My wasting days shall sound thy praise	62	79
My soul, shake off thy gloomy fears	87	109
Mine eyes, behold the rising sun	103	131
My God, to thee for help I fly	108	137
My God, my everlasting hope	128	165
My God, my Saviour, and my King	ib	166

N

	Page	Hymn
Now, dearest Lord, to praise thy name	14	9
No temple ever built by art	23	24
Now floating waves and billows roar	37	45

O

	Page	Hymn
Our wasting days are rolling on	19	16
Our sorrows and desponding fears	42	51
O God, before thy mercy-seat	57	72
O thou who, when I did complain	57	73
Our doubting fears and flowing tears	63	81
O death! unnumber'd are thy slain	72	93
O God! thou bottomless abyss	77	99
O how ought mortal man to live	81	103
On thee, each morning, O my God	91	114
O God, in mercy hear my pray'r	ib	115
O ye! who foreign climes explore	105	133
O thou, who from my infant years	116	148
O thou high thron'd above all height	122	156
O come, let us join in music divine	124	160
Once more my soul the rising day	136	175

R

	Page	Hymn
Rejoice ye ransom'd sons of men	35	42

Salvation,

S	Page	Hymn
Salvation, O the joyful sound	21	19
Sweet is the mem'ry of thy grace	34	41
Shall the vile race of flesh and blood	59	75
See, gracious God, before thy throne	123	158

T	Page	Hymn
The undesigning hand of chance	22	22
The morning flow'rs display their sweets	23	25
Thee Jesus, full of truth and peace	36	44
Thee we adore, eternal name	38	46
Thou King of nations, who ordain'st	40	49
Thy works of glory, mighty Lord	45	56
Think, O my soul, devoutly think	46	58
The spacious firmament on high	48	60
Thy praise, O God, I'll found abroad	51	65
To heav'n I lift my waiting eyes	55	70
The Sun of Righteousness appears	64	82
To praise the Lord with one accord	66	85
Terrible thought, shall I alone	71	92
The fiery contest now is o'er	73	95
Thou Son of God, whose flaming eyes	80	102
Thou didst, O mighty God, exist	84	106
Thou dwell'st, O God, in radiant flame	92	116
Thrice happy are the souls that mourn	93	117
The sacred pages of thy word	99	125
To thee, O God, I hourly sigh	104	132
Thou Judge of quick and dead	107	136
Thy heav'nly blessings, dearest Lord	109	138
Thou who a servant didst become	110	140
The morn is past, the noon-tide o'er	111	141
Tho' troubles assail, and dangers affright	112	142
Thrice blessed are the humble hearts	117	149
'Twas God that tun'd the rolling spheres	119	152
To him whose mercy thro' the day	120	153
Thou, sacred spring of life, before thine eyes	121	155
To thee, my God, my gracious King	137	176

W	Page	Hymn
When unrelenting justice cry'd	15	10
When the last angel's trump shall sound	28	32

When

	Page	Hymn
When in the roaring lion's teeth	31	26
When rising from the bed of death	49	62
Who shall inhabit in thy hill	52	66
What mortal can entirely scan	53	67
Wasting days are rolling on	54	69
With meekness and humility	60	76
When I the sacred tomb behold	ib	77
While our Redeemer here abode	76	98
Wherewith shall I approach the Lord	93	118
When quiet in my house I sit	116	147
While thee I seek, protecting pow'r	133	173

Y

	Page	Hymn
Ye thoughtless tribes, whose glowing cheek	63	80
Ye virgin souls, arise	85	108

AN

ALPHABETICAL TABLE,

CONTAINING

An Explanation of such words in the foregoing pages as the common reader may be unacquainted with.

A
Abyss, a bottomless pit
Adamantine, hard, inflexible
Adulation, flattery
Alternative, the choice out of two
Amber, a yellow transparent substance
Ambient, surrounding
Amphitheatre, a building of a circular or oval form
Annals, histories written in order of time
Animated, spirited, lively
Antidate, to date before the time, or to enjoy a thing in imagination before it exists
Anticipate, to take up before the time
Antiquated, worn out, old
Apace, quickly
Architect, a chief builder
Artist, a professor of an art
Assiduous, constant in application
Atoms, small particles
Attractive, inviting
Aurora, the morning
Auxiliary, helping, assistant

B
Bastion, a bulwark
Beamy, shining
Behest, command, order
Belles, handsome young girls
Blab, to tell a secret, to tattle
Bland, soft, mild
Blandishments, soft words
Blended, mixed
Blighted, blasted
Board, a table
Boon, a gift, favour
Boreas, the north wind
Brine, the sea
Buffoon, a man that practises indecent raillery

C
Callow, wanting feathers, naked
Cants, barbarous jargon
Car, a cart, chariot
Caveat, warning
Cell, a cave, a small close room, &c.
Chaos, confusion
Choir, a set of singers
Chink, a small opening
Chymist, a philosopher by fire
Cite,

Cite, summons
Circumscribe, to inclose, limit, or confine
Clarify, to make clean, clear, &c.
Clime, a tract of land
Compunction, repentance
Concave, hollow as the inner curve of an arch
Congeal'd, frozen
Coincide, to agree with
Convulsed, violently agitated
Coral, a plant of a stony nature growing in the water
Courtly, polite
Cozenage, deceit, fraud
Credulity, easiness of belief
Crimination, accusation
Cynic, having the qualities of a dog, currish, brutal snarling, satyrical
Cynthia, the moon

D

Demagogue, the ringleader of a rabble
Demons, evil spirits
Despotic, absolute, unlimited
Disembodied, divested of a body
Disjoined, separated
Diurnal, daily
Drizzling, falling in small drops
Dub, to confer an honour
Dun'd, troubled, teased

E

Ebriety, drunkenness
Elate, flushed with success
Elude, to avoid by artifice

Emanation, that which issues from another substance
Emblems, representations
Empyrean, the highest heavens
Emulate, to imitate with a view of equality
Entail, an estate unalterably settled
Environed, surrounded
Epicure, one given to luxury
Ethereal, heavenly
Evade, to shift, escape
Exit, departure, death
Exhalations, fumes, steams, vapours
Expanse, a widely extended body
Expanding, opening
Explode, to reject with scorn
Explore, to examine
Extorted, forced
Exulting, rejoicing

F

Fend, to defend
Fiat, command
Filial, belonging to a son
Flagicious, wicked
Fluid, not solid
Foibles, failings
Foplings, petty fops
Forager, a plunderer
Function, employment

G

Gait, manner of air, walking
Gems, jewels
Genial, fruitful
Guise, manner, dress
Glides, flows silently
Goal,

Goal, prison, final purpose, or starting post
Guardian, a protector

H

Hector, a quarrelsome fellow
Herald, a forerunner, officer
Hierarchies, chiefs of the sacred order
Hooted, despised

I

Illicit, unlawful, improper
Imbecillity, weakness
Immur'd, shut in, imprisoned
Impelled, forced, urged
Impending, hanging over, near at hand
Implore, to ask, beg
Impregnant, to make fruitful
Impulse, communicated force
Inactive, idle, at rest
Infringed, violated
Insatiate, greedy, so as not to be satisfied
Insolvent, unable to pay debts
Intellect, the power of understanding, knowledge
Intelligential, consisting of mind free from body
Intercepts, stops, hinders
Internal, inward
Intricate, perplexed, entangled
Invectives, railing speeches

L

Labyrinth, a place formed with intricate windings
Lambkins, little lambs
Landscape, a view of a country

Languid, feeble, heartless
Latent, hidden, secret
Lays, songs
Legions, vast numbers
Libertines, bad men
Limpid, clear, pure
Lyre, a musical instrument

M

Magnetic, drawing
Malignant, malicious
Matron, a grave elderly woman
Matin, morning
Maze, a confusion of mind
Menial, a servant
Mental, existing in the mind
Meridian, at the point of noon, southern
Mien, air, look, manner
Mirrors, looking-glasses
Modish, fashionable, airy, gay
Mood, temper of mind
Morpheus, the god of sleep or dreams
Mute, silent, not speaking

N

Nymph, a goddess of the woods, meadows, or waters, in poetry it signifies a lady

O

Obnoxious, liable, subject
Obvious, plain, evident
Orbs, spheres, circles, celestial bodies, planets
Ore, metal unrefined
Orient, eastern
Outbrave, bear down, dare

Y. Peasant,

P

Pallid, pale, wan
Peasant, a country man
Pendant, hanging over
Permanent, lasting
Phantom, a fancied vision
Phœnix, a bird which is supposed to exist single, and to arise again out of its own ashes
Philanthropic, loving mankind
Pines, trees
Plaintive, sorrowful
Plastic, having the power to give form
Plume, to pride one's self
Plumy, feathered
Poignant, sharp, severe
Poize, to balance, weigh
Polemic, controversial
Poles, points about which the earth turns
Ponderous, weighty
Portals, gates
Portend, foretoken
Potable, that may be drunk
Potentate, a sovereign
Pother, bustle, stir
Prescient, foreknowing
Precluded, shut out
Precipitance, rash haste
Pregnant, full, fertile, clear
Primeval, such as was at first
Pristine, original, ancient
Privation, loss or destruction
Progeny, offspring
Progressive, going forward
Protract, to lengthen out
Purloin, to pilfer, steal
Pyramids, square pillars ending in a point

Q

Quaff, to drink hard

R

Radiant, sparkling, shining
Redundent, superfluous, over much
Refulgent, glittering, splendid, bright
Reined, restrained
Reptile, creeping on many feet
Repugnant, opposite, contrary
Romantic, irregular, wild, desert
Rotation, whirling round like a wheel, a course or turn
Rote, words said without meaning

S

Sable, black, dark
Sages, men of wisdom
Sanguine, forward, warm
Satanic, devilish, infernal
Scan, to examine
Scars, marks of cutting
Sculptured, carved
Scutcheon, the ground on which a coat of arms is painted
Sectarean, opposite to things established
Seers, prophets, wise men
Sequestered, remote, distant, set aside
Serpentine,

Serpentine, winding like a serpent
Sire, father, title of kings
Solar, being of, or belonging to the sun
Sorded, base, mean
Spangled, shining
Spectre, an apparition
Spright, a spirit shade
Spurious, not genuine, counterfeit
Statics, the science of weighing bodies
Stigmatize, to brand with infamy
Streaks, rays, lines of colours
Supernal, heavenly
Sway, power, authority
System, method, theory

T
Tapestry, a cloth woven in figures, hangings
Tend, to keep or attend
Terrene, earthly
Terrestrial, earthly
Test, trial, means of trial
Tinged, coloured
Towers, which rises high
Trappings, trifling decorations
Transparent, bright
Triune, three in one
Trivial, trifling
Turret, a little tower

U
Variegated, different colours
Vassal, a subject, slave
Vegitate, to grow as plants
Vindictive, revengeful
Verdant, green, flourishing
Vernal, blooming
Vicegerent, one acting by substitution for another
Victim, a sacrifice
Vital, necessary to life
Vivacious, gay, lively
Uncouth, odd, awkward
Unction, ointment
Unrelenting, hard, cruel
Untutor'd, untaught
Urbanity, civility, elegance
Urn, a vessel used for the ashes of the dead, &c.

W
Warded, turned aside
Wild, *noun*, a desert
Welkin, the visible region of the air, the sky
Woodbines, a shrub

Z
Zephyrs, the west wind

FINIS.

www.ingramcontent.com/pod-product-compliance
Lightning Source LLC
Chambersburg PA
CBHW032146230426
43672CB00011B/2464